Contents

ONE

Introduction to Headhunting

Everyone has the potential to be 'headhunted'. This is the process of being approached either directly by your current employer or an external employer, or indirectly by a headhunting agency or through a contact, about a particular position. Whether or not it happens to you depends upon how much time, effort and energy you are prepared to devote to 'networking' (making useful contacts), building your professional reputation and promoting yourself.

You are your own press officer and have the power to influence the people around you. You – not others – are in charge of your career, so focus on what you want from your life in the future and then plan for it. Planning will help you to reduce your dependence on outside events and will make you more responsible for yourself and the direction your life takes. It can lead you to greater career fulfilment as you reach the milestones and targets that you set yourself instead of drifting from job to job, never looking further than a couple of years into the future. Whatever you want, it is up to you to achieve it.

Being headhunted is therefore not just for the privileged few: it is for all those people who can take charge of their career and promote themselves in areas where others will notice, value and then recruit those with a professional reputation.

You deserve the best, and this book will teach you how to create the best career opportunities for yourself by knocking on the right doors – doors which will open up new and exciting opportunities for you.

The importance of reputation

A reputation consists of those things for which a person is well known and valued, or in which he/she is deemed to be an expert. You need to have a reputation in order to be attractive to employers and headhunting agencies, as it is this that distinguishes you from the competition, sells you and eventually determines your market rate (salary). You therefore need to build up a respected reputation which can be backed up by facts and figures, achievements, personal successes and the support of others, and given a bit of time and effort this can be accomplished. In Chapter 2 you will have the opportunity to assess your current reputation, while Chapter 3 demonstrates how to build and maintain a worthy business reputation. The business world survives and thrives on reputations, so never underestimate their importance. An organization's reputation affects its performance, its position in the marketplace and its capacity to win new business, and is built up by the individual people who work for it. There is thus no escape from the concept of reputation, and *your* reputation is vital to your future success.

REPUTATION AND CANDIDATE SELECTION

Reputations are assessed regularly – probably more regularly than you would care to imagine. Up and down the country, companies constantly look to fill jobs, and day after day managers put together lists of internal candidates to fill any vacant positions. These lists are based upon each person's capabilities, experiences, achievements, personality and vision for the future – in short, upon their work reputation and the team's perception of this reputation. Such internal selection decisions are therefore sometimes based on less information than that which appears on a CV. In addition, in choosing candidates a manager's own reputation is on the line, so he/she does not want to select someone who could let the company down, fail to perform in the job, or who would not be respected by his/her colleagues.

So, selection of the right person is crucial. However, when choosing internal candidates a team of managers will tend to come up with the same names for certain job profiles, and often in the same order. In fact, 95 per cent of people aren't even considered, and it is normally possible to count the proposed candidates on the fingers of one hand. In practice, a team will very quickly come up with a list of three names – and will then often widen the net to include around 10 names because they feel that there must be more than just three!

The next step is to select the right person for the job. To do this, the team will tap into the company's network: either indirectly, by talking to the manager of the preferred candidate, or directly, by approaching the shortlisted candidate him/herself. However, it is rare for the 'direct' approach to be all that direct, and the research is usually carried out in a cryptic manner by asking relatively vague questions – such as 'Do you know anyone who would be interested in this position?', 'How would you feel about doing such and such?', 'What is your position over . . . ?' – in order to assess the person's response and attitude. Remember that people reveal a lot about themselves, their career aspirations and their attitude when they are off their guard, so try to regard all conversations as important and try to portray a positive image of yourself at all times.

External job selections rely heavily on a candidate's reputation. Prospective employers will also carry out a lot of investigative work by speaking to their contacts, the current employer or anyone who knows the candidate. Focus on building a positive reputation and your career opportunities will increase accordingly.

Being headhunted

People who have been approached and later appointed by a headhunter have said that it was:

- Flattering, a huge compliment.

- Prestigious, exciting.

- Classy, a sign of being one of the elite.

- Different, unusual, scary.

- Expected.

- Unexpected, surprising – why me?

- Good to be wanted.

- Recognition of the highest kind.

People thus have a range of different reactions to the concept of a headhunter pursuing them for a job, but common to all is the element of sheer *pride*: the feeling that someone, somewhere has been watching them and has recognized their personal qualities and successes to date. Some people have even gone so far as to say that it was like being famous, even if only for a very short period of time! On the whole, the responses tend to be of a positive rather than a negative or defensive nature. In fact, people's reactions demonstrate that nothing beats the power of being chosen – handpicked and selected – rather than simply appointed in the usual way.

A call from a headhunter will do your ego the world of good and you have every right to feel proud of yourself. It is normal to crave recognition and praise for your achievements, and nothing is more powerful than public recognition. However, you should avoid letting it go to your head. Keep your feet firmly on the ground and remember the following:

- **A call is only a call**. Many people fall into the trap of thinking that a call from a headhunter means that they have actually got the job. Of course, they haven't – this is only the beginning of an episode which may or may not lead eventually to an offer.

- **Keep the information to yourself.** Avoid jeopardizing your current position and future prospects by talking to others about how you have been approached by a head-hunter. People are not impressed by being told how suc-cessful you are, and conceit of this sort rarely wins you many friends. In fact, you may well bruise a few egos and turn other people against you, who could then make life difficult by spreading rumours that your loyalties no longer lie with your current company, thereby damaging your reputation, and perhaps even steal your opportunities.

Instead, remember that everyone has an ego that they protect and nurture, and which you should avoid threatening at all costs. In fact, other people's egos are your allies, so learn to value them. No one will ever do something because you want them to do it – they will only do what they want to do – so if you can respect and understand other people and avoid challenging them it will be easier for you to work and do business with them.

Try to observe how other people behave. This will give you an insight into what is important to them, and it will then be far easier for you to predict how they will behave in certain business situations. Learn to focus on the situation and its importance rather than on the effect that it has on your ego. Be conscious of your own ego. How important is it to you? Do you have to be the best, or are you prepared to share the limelight with others? Try to become aware of your own strengths and weaknesses. You should make an effort to avoid becoming so self-orientated that you fail to notice or value other people. It is far easier to get on with colleagues if you can relate to what is important to them rather than always considering only what is most important to you.

- **Always select rather than accept a job.** Never, never take a job solely because you have been headhunted for it. It has to be the right job and career move for you, so stick by your principles and don't be afraid to turn something down – after all, if it is not right, you will not be throwing anything away.

  In these circumstances, bear in mind that if you can help by suggesting the names of people who might be interested in the job you should do so. Highlight the person's strengths, experience to date, and past successes *honestly*, for whatever messages you send out, they will eventually come back to you. You should therefore never be afraid to sing someone else's praises, for it will be only a matter of time before someone is doing the same for you.

Time management

Time is important as far as a career is concerned. Some people expect instant career success, while others are prepared to work to achieve success. Time management has a lot to do with your expectations about a particular job or task, so if you can change your perception of time you can frequently change your whole attitude to work, and this – in turn – can improve your performance and your prospects.

Very often my clients say that they don't have the time to carry out the procedures suggested in this book in order to increase their potential for being headhunted. Everyone's time is limited, so it is vital that you learn to value it (a doctor friend of mine once told me that people on their death bed rarely say that they wish they'd had more money, but they often say that they wish they'd spent more time with their family). At certain points in their lives, most people have probably felt that they could do with having more time; in addition most people have probably said to themselves on occasion that they will attend to the priorities first and then they'll have the time to do other tasks, but very often when the time arrives to do these other things they find they are too exhausted. So what is the answer?

The answer lies in the way you perceive the time to do your jobs and the time to enjoy. People tend to have paradigms of time: for example, they may have structured work time and then structured home/social time, so that their lives are divided into work, leisure and family/social life. This may sound all too familiar to you. Most people like to have structured time, as it makes them feel comfortable and secure, and in fact there is nothing wrong with having a structured and organized life, but you should avoid being governed by time. Do you do things out of force of habit rather than because you want to do them? A simple example would be having a cup of coffee at 10am because it is coffee time rather than because you are actually thirsty. Instead, you need to strike a balance between the activity and the time.

So, activity primarily needs to be constructive and positive rather than merely something to pass the time. If you adopt this approach, your time will be used in a much more rewarding and fulfilling way.

BENEFITS OF TIME MANAGEMENT

If you were told that you had only six months left to live, what would you do? Would you spend your limited time feeling angry and sorry for yourself, or would you want to do certain positive things? The purpose of this exercise is not to get you feeling morbid, but to make you focus and think about *what is important to you.*

If something is important to you, then don't ignore it. Spend time doing whatever it is, and you will benefit by feeling more alive as a person, and less frustrated and resentful – and you will probably find more time to do all those other things as well! Most people, however, don't manage their time in this way. They spend most of it filling in time and getting distracted from the important issues by:

✗ Moaning.

✗ Thinking negatively.

✗ Daydreaming.

✗ Thinking in the past.

✗ Criticizing themselves or others.

✗ Failing to say 'No'.

✗ Getting pressurized or bullied into things.

✗ Having too many projects on the go.

However, if you manage your time you are unlikely to fall into these traps, because you will be fulfilling yourself in the present. In relation to your career, you will be able to concentrate on:

✔ Your image.

✔ Your reputation and profession.

✔ What is important to you.

✔ The present.

✔ Letting your reputation lead the way.

Resist the temptation to fill your time and start to focus on the important issues rather than on everything else (see pages 39–41). Time never stands still, and unless you learn to manage your time there is always the possibility of *never* finding the time to do something you want to. If you can manage your time, your career will sail with the wind rather than against it. This means that you will be able to choose between opportunities rather than seeking them for yourself or simply holding on to your job (see Figure 1). Rise above the rest and use your time to create the best possible career opportunities for yourself.

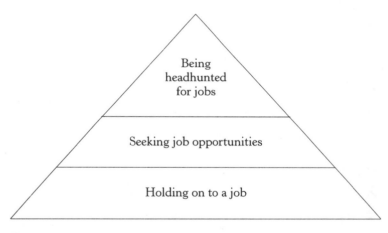

Rising to opportunities

Being
headhunted
for jobs

Seeking job opportunities

Holding on to a job

Figure 1

THIS BOOK WILL DEMONSTRATE

1 How to assess and improve your headhunting potential.

2 How to value your own key assets.

3 How to build your reputation and become a specialist within your field of work.

4 How to promote your experience and expertise externally by networking, writing articles, appearing in the media and mixing with other people within the same profession.

5 How to observe and watch others so that you understand the person before you communicate with them, in order to develop good business relationships.

6 How to manage and maximize the use of your time.

7 How to improve your job performance and the quality of your output.

8 How to improve your attitude and physical well-being, which may be hindering your career progress.

9 How to prepare a CV and develop interview technique in order to promote yourself on to a headhunter's shortlist of candidates.

10 How to respond to the procedures of the headhunter in a professional manner.

11 How to promote yourself internally within your current company into the next job.

12 Finally, this book will demonstrate the benefits of headhunting and show how it can increase your career options dramatically. Follow the procedures laid out in this book and it will be only a matter of time before someone will telephone you. Good luck.

TWO

Assessing Your Current Profile

The questionnaire in this chapter is designed to help you assess your potential to be headhunted, to show you where your strengths and weaknesses lie, and to highlight the areas for improvement. It therefore stresses the importance of having an all-round, sound and versatile profile within your profession. The questionnaire will help you to think beyond simply having a job and getting a new one, and to work towards attracting employers who will seek you out for their job opening. It will help you to:

- Realize that everything you do or don't do in a job is important.

- Understand the key areas of importance for an employer.

- Realize that your attitude to work, social activities and life in general are important.

- Finally, following the recommendations appropriate to your overall score in the questionnaire will coach you in how to be headhunted.

If you want to achieve a career which puts you in the limelight you will have to work at it. The first challenges are to become a committed and key person at what you do; to create and develop an image that is suitable for public life; to promote yourself in the right areas; to respect other people and different cultures; and to display a professional attitude at all times. Have a go at completing the questionnaire: you may be pleasantly surprised to learn that you are on the right track and that it is just a matter of fine tuning in a few areas. However, if you discover that you have a lot of work to do, do not despair – at least you now know what is required in order for you to get on to the career fast track. A tip worth remembering is that if something has worked particularly well for you up to now, then recognize it and continue to do whatever it is. Above all, this questionnaire is designed to show you that what you may previously have considered to be a hurdle no longer has to be regarded as one – so complete it without delay.

The questionnaire

The questionnaire overleaf is divided into ten sections. Under each section there are a number of statements for you to consider. To complete the questionnaire, rate your performance, capability or expertise in each of the areas listed by deciding whether it is excellent (5), good (3), poor (1) or a liability (0). The key is to give an honest answer which truly reflects your abilities. Otherwise, you will be kidding no one but yourself.

How do you rate your abilities in the following areas?

Decision-making

1   *Recognize when a decision has to be made.* `SCORE [____]`

2   *Know when to refer a decision.* `SCORE [____]`

3   *Weigh up and calculate the options.* `SCORE [____]`

4   *Assess the risk factors.* `SCORE [____]`

5   *Persuade others to your way of thinking.* `SCORE [____]`

6   *Make a timely decision.* `SCORE [____]`

7   *Voice constructive objections to a possible decision.* `SCORE [____]`

8   *Support others, follow the party line and avoid criticizing the decision afterwards.* `SCORE [____]`

9   *Take ownership of your decisions.* `SCORE [____]`

10 *Have the courage to reverse a wrong decision.* `SCORE [____]`

11 *Evaluate and learn from previous decisions.* `SCORE [____]`

12 *Recognize and compliment others on a decision well taken.* `SCORE [____]`

English

1   *Reading and comprehension.*   `SCORE ____`

2   *Spelling, grammar and sentence construction.*   `SCORE ____`

3   *Express yourself concisely and succinctly.*   `SCORE ____`

4   *Use a range of vocabulary.*   `SCORE ____`

5   *Write in different styles.*   `SCORE ____`

6   *Write under pressure.*   `SCORE ____`

7   *Have an understanding of current affairs.*   `SCORE ____`

8   *Talk on a subject without forcing your opinions on someone else.*   `SCORE ____`

9   *Use clichés and quotes correctly and effectively.*   `SCORE ____`

10   *Summarize and paraphrase.*   `SCORE ____`

11   *Have an understanding of other people's opinions, however difficult it might be.*   `SCORE ____`

12   *Proofread and correct written material.*   `SCORE ____`

13   *Write up minutes.*   `SCORE ____`

14   *Explore the views of others without prejudice by asking how, what, when and where rather than why.*   `SCORE ____`

SCORING: EXCELLENT 5, GOOD 3, POOR 1, LIABILITY 0

Attending meetings

1   *Arrive on time.* `SCORE ___`

2   *Prepare beforehand and take any notes, overheads or other material with you.* `SCORE ___`

3   *Take the necessary files and information and draw out the appropriate paperwork when requested.* `SCORE ___`

4   *Remain focused throughout the meeting, avoiding distraction techniques such as tidying up the desk or paperwork, walking around the room, putting feet up on the desk or talking about social issues.* `SCORE ___`

5   *Remain alert throughout the meeting and avoid yawning, fidgeting or sliding back in the chair.* `SCORE ___`

6   *Work towards the meeting's objectives through consensus rather than sidetracking, power talking or confrontation.* `SCORE ___`

7   *Take ownership of your agreed action points and avoid leaving them half done or, worse still, not done at all.* `SCORE ___`

8   *Actively listen to other people and build upon what has been said, rather than talking without thinking, finishing other people's sentences and second guessing what someone is saying.* `SCORE ___`

9   *Decline meetings where your involvement or contribution is minimal or next to nothing.* `SCORE ___`

10   *Know when to remain silent in order to avoid re-discussing what has already been said or being drawn into discussions which are outside your responsibility, knowledge or authority.* `SCORE ___`

SCORING: EXCELLENT 5, GOOD 3, POOR 1, LIABILITY 0

Chairing meetings

1   Determine when a meeting should or should not
be called.   SCORE

2   Choose the people with the appropriate skills
and expertise.   SCORE

3   Prepare a comprehensive, clear and detailed
agenda and circulate it well in advance.   SCORE

4   Organize a suitable date and time, and a venue
with appropriate facilities.   SCORE

5   Establish clearly at the beginning of the meeting
its objectives and purpose, and highlight what is
expected from the participants.   SCORE

6   Visualize in advance what success will look like.   SCORE

7   Chair, manage and direct the discussions in
accordance with the objectives.   SCORE

8   Summarize throughout the meeting the points
discussed, and assign responsibility for action
points.   SCORE

9   Control time carefully while ensuring open and fair
discussions, and complete within the allotted time.   SCORE

10   Regularly assess and ask for feedback on your
ability to chair meetings.   SCORE

Presentations

1   Prepare an interesting, thoughtful and
appropriate presentation.

SCORE [____]

2   Find the time to rehearse aloud beforehand.

SCORE [____]

3   Deliver your presentation with interest, using a
variety of pace, pitch and tone.

SCORE [____]

4   Complete your presentation within the
allotted time.

SCORE [____]

5   Keep the audience interested and alert and involve
them when necessary. (Remember that if the
audience has no questions for you at the end, then
you have either bored them or baffled them!)

SCORE [____]

6   Change your style to avoid giving the same
presentation on the same material over and
over again.

SCORE [____]

7   Understand your audience and tailor your
presentation accordingly.

SCORE [____]

8   Present to audiences varying in both numbers and
technical ability.

SCORE [____]

9   Prepare appropriate hand-outs which are
available on the day.

SCORE [____]

10   Listen to feedback and take the necessary actions.

SCORE [____]

Technical expertise

1   *Talk in meetings on and around your subject and
    speciality, rather than simply for the sake of
    talking.*   SCORE ____

2   *Keep up-to-date with the latest legislation
    affecting your profession and ultimately your job.*   SCORE ____

3   *Spend time continuously learning, retraining and
    reading your professional journals and magazines.*   SCORE ____

4   *Communicate your messages confidently to people
    who know less than you do, to people of the same
    technical ability, and to people more senior and
    with more expertise than yourself.*   SCORE ____

5   *Recognize people who are more knowledgeable
    than you and be open enough to learn from them.*   SCORE ____

6   *Be able to talk both seriously and with a sense
    of humour.*   SCORE ____

7   *Be able to stand back from a situation, distance
    yourself from the emotional aspects and seek the
    optimum ways of solving the problem.*   SCORE ____

8   *Be able to apply your speciality practically and
    gain experience in it, rather than just being seen
    as a theorist on the subject.*   SCORE ____

9   *Have confidence in yourself and your abilities,
    and therefore be able to choose the right moment or
    time to carry out whatever it is you want to do,
    suggest or change.*   SCORE ____

10 *Stand your ground in the face of opposition,
    based on your competence, common sense and
    mastery of the subject.*   SCORE ____

SCORING: EXCELLENT 5, GOOD 3, POOR 1, LIABILITY 0

Assertiveness

1   *Express yourself and your positive feelings easily and freely.*

`SCORE`

2   *Change your mind.*

`SCORE`

3   *Say 'No' to other people when you feel it is appropriate, rather than saying 'Yes' and then feel guilty or resentful afterwards.*

`SCORE`

4   *Carry out actions which you believe are right despite how they may be interpreted by others.*

`SCORE`

5   *Take responsibility for actions rather than avoid or delegate what you don't want to do.*

`SCORE`

6   *Put your point across in a professional manner, rather than getting aggressive or staying quiet and then becoming passively aggressive.*

`SCORE`

7   *Feel happy and relish opportunities given to you, rather than feeling guilty or embarrassed about your good fortune.*

`SCORE`

8   *Give credit to others where credit is due, and recognize and use other people's skills and qualities.*

`SCORE`

9   *Feel comfortable with being chosen to manage current colleagues or friends.*

`SCORE`

10   *Have the confidence to challenge senior management on issues you disagree with.*

`SCORE`

11   *Ask for additional help, resources and time when necessary, rather than struggling on alone.*

`SCORE`

SCORING: EXCELLENT 5, GOOD 3, POOR 1, LIABILITY 0

12 *Regularly request performance feedback from your boss, actively listen to his/her comments and take action accordingly.*

SCORE ⬜

13 *Take time to coach subordinates, allowing them to be less dependent in the future.*

SCORE ⬜

14 *Have confidence in a subordinate's abilities and believe that they can perform a job as well as or better than yourself.*

SCORE ⬜

15 *Recruit a person who is right for the job rather than someone who is in a similar mould to yourself.*

SCORE ⬜

16 *Promptly bring to a subordinate's notice jobs that are performed below standard – without bullying or destroying the person's confidence.*

SCORE ⬜

17 *Give a subordinate the flexibility to use his/her own judgement and creativity.*

SCORE ⬜

18 *Openly welcome a subordinate's good performance without regarding it as a threat to yourself.*

SCORE ⬜

SCORING: EXCELLENT 5, GOOD 3, POOR 1, LIABILITY 0

Personal life

1 Combine business and personal life so that you
   avoid role conflict and have a life, not just a job. `SCORE`

2 Have interests outside work, so that there is a
   balance between work and personal life. `SCORE`

3 Understand your stress levels and be able to
   release stress. `SCORE`

4 Be able to share business emotions, crises, concerns
   and triumphs with someone outside work. `SCORE`

5 Have enough 'self' time in order to refresh, restore
   and revitalize yourself. `SCORE`

6 Take full allocation of holiday leave. `SCORE`

7 Maintain a clean and reputable lifestyle in order to
   avoid any skeletons in the cupboard or potential
   embarrassments. `SCORE`

8 Talk on a variety of subjects other than just work. `SCORE`

9 Manage your personal finances in order to avoid
   over-burdening yourself. `SCORE`

10 Have a supportive spouse/partner who shares
   rather than threatens your objectives and
   aspirations. `SCORE`

SCORING: EXCELLENT 5, GOOD 3, POOR 1, LIABILITY 0

Image

1   Understand how others view and label you.   `SCORE`

2   Recognize that your image may need to be changed or modified.   `SCORE`

3   Identify and decide upon the image you want to portray.   `SCORE`

4   Establish a consistent image and continuously communicate it to others.   `SCORE`

5   Avoid blunders, sleaze and criticism – the very things that could tarnish your image.   `SCORE`

6   Avoid repetition of facts, sentences or stories, which could allow others to relabel you.   `SCORE`

7   Avoid using embarrassing, humorous or unpleasant gestures, such as running in the corridor, picking spots or having a crushing hand shake!   `SCORE`

8   Recognize and adhere to the required business etiquette.   `SCORE`

9   Portray an individual rather than a stereotyped image.   `SCORE`

10   Listen to your common sense to do what is right rather than what may seem a good option.   `SCORE`

SCORING: EXCELLENT 5, GOOD 3, POOR 1, LIABILITY 0

Networking

1   *Know people within your profession whom you can use to give you advice.* `SCORE`

2   *Keep in contact with people on a regular basis, rather than only contacting them when you want something.* `SCORE`

3   *Make the effort to meet people in person on their territory, rather than just talking to them over the phone or writing to them.* `SCORE`

4   *Be interested in and show an understanding of other people, rather than viewing a meeting as an opportunity for you to talk to them about yourself.* `SCORE`

5   *Be interested in the 'whole' person rather than just the business part of them, so that you know what is important to them.* `SCORE`

6   *Formally congratulate people on their achievements and announcements.* `SCORE`

7   *View networking as a business opportunity rather than as a chore or distraction.* `SCORE`

8   *Have a good memory for people's names.* `SCORE`

9   *Avoid being regarded as a social climber because you only bother with those senior to you.* `SCORE`

10   *Avoid being seen as 'one of the boys/girls' because you only mix with people on a par with or below you.* `SCORE`

SCORING: EXCELLENT 5, GOOD 3, POOR 1, LIABILITY 0

SCORING

When you have completed the questionnaire, add up all the numbers to arrive at your total score.

Up to 200

In many of the sections you have scored below average. Refer to each section to pinpoint where the gaps lie, then focus on improving one section at a time to avoid becoming discouraged. Remember that everyone should be technically competent and a specialist in their chosen field, so concentrate on this first – knowledge is power.

Up to 400

A good score, but there is still room for improvement. To be noticed and therefore headhunted you have to do more than just carry out your job, so focus on excelling in your role.

Over 400

An excellent score, which indicates that you either have been or are likely to be headhunted. Continue to develop your skills as you progress through your career. However, do remember that work can dominate your life if you let it, so it is important to learn how to 'switch off' at weekends and on holiday. Work when it is necessary – which at times may be up to 24 hours a day or over a weekend – but when you are not working, stop and switch off. This can be difficult, given modern technology such as mobile phones, fax and e-mail. However, when you go away, although you should always leave a phone number, do encourage subordinates and colleagues to take responsibility themselves. This is an essential business skill which will make you a far more valuable asset to any organization.

THREE

Becoming an Expert in Your Field

Experts are a valuable asset to any organization, for these people have a wealth of technical and practical experience, an eye for detail, and can perform their job with minimal supervision. They can carry out every aspect of their job and understand how it fits into the organization as a whole. They can also draw upon previous experiences and situations, and can use this knowledge to make the right judgements and decisions in accordance with current requirements. In short, an expert gains the admiration and support of others because he/she doesn't simply perform the job but *excels* in it.

Experts are hard to come by and because of this they are sought after and rewarded accordingly. Even though most people appreciate the importance of being a specialist in their field they do not fall into this category, because although they may be good at what they do, they are not an expert at it. People often do only part of a job well, or they shy away from the detail, or they move on before they have learned or performed fully within the job. A reputation of this sort is therefore not as solid as it could be. This chapter will show you how to build your professional reputation, based on becoming an expert and promoting your expertise, which in turn will greatly enhance your prospects of being headhunted.

The onus is on you to own, build and promote your reputation, as no one else will do it for you. You are responsible for your job and career, but there are no guarantees as to how it will all turn out. However, if you follow the simple procedure outlined in this chapter you will increase your opportunities for advancement, new challenges, recognition and fulfilment.

Building your reputation involves:

- Becoming an expert.

- Putting in a quality performance.

- Managing your time.

- Avoiding the common pitfalls.

By focusing your energy and efforts in these areas you will perform a valuable role and in doing so earn the respect of those around you. Remember: value and respect build a worthy reputation.

Becoming an expert

Whether you like it or not, your job performance will be assessed continuously – people are judged on what they do in a job, rather than on what they meant to do or should have done.

It is not as difficult as it might appear to become an expert. Until you become one, you will always be at a disadvantage and to some extent an outsider, for if you are not up to date and do not know all your stuff, you will not be so influential and proactive within the organization. People will not call on you to offer your opinion or take your advice, so you will be required more to implement other people's instructions and procedures than to put your own ideas into practice. This can make you feel powerless and resentful; if you don't want to fall into this trap, you must recognize the importance of knowledge, for knowledge is power and power brings greater freedom, choice and opportunities. Your best course of action, therefore, is to focus on becoming an expert.

ESTABLISHING A TRADEMARK

A trademark is a phrase, sentence or a few words associated with you. Everyone has a trademark, so if you are unaware of yours it has probably been invented for you by others – and it may not be all that flattering! To become an expert, you need to have a trademark which communicates where your expertise lies, for example: 'So and so is an expert in risk management'; 'he/she is a whiz on the computer'; or 'he/she is an expert at project development'. A trademark is thus a short sentence which describes your unique branding, value to an organization and can be recognized easily by others.

People create their own trademarks. They do this by communicating, normally subconsciously, their positive or negative message to the outside world. If a person has a positive trademark, he/she has achieved that by relaying positive and beneficial messages; similarly, if a person has a negative trademark, he/she has gained that by giving out negative messages. These messages are then picked up and used later by others: the individual becomes 'labelled' in a certain light, and the trademark can then become firmly cast in concrete in people's minds so that is it difficult for others to see the person in any other way. Labelling is very common and most people are guilty of it, because it makes them feel comfortable, secure and less threatened by others. The key, therefore, is to create and promote your own positive label.

What is your trademark? Are you aware of what people say about you, either directly or behind your back? To establish what your trademark is, you need to do several things.

❶ Recall what your manager said about you at your recent appraisal. Were you labelled by what you do and have done, or by how you behave? This is an important question, because sometimes a person's behaviour is predominant over their actions. Under these circumstances, they often unknowingly invite criticism because their attitude is either inappropriate, immature or selfish. You may have ignored or argued with your manager, or even taken to heart what was said about you, but the key with criticism is how you perceive it.

Try to view criticism as positive and as an opportunity to learn something new about yourself. In order to take positive action, try to avoid reacting to what has been said or holding on to the anger, annoyance or hurt. Instead, distance yourself from the emotion and who has said what, for that is not important, and focus on what was actually said, holding it in your mind and thinking about it for a while.

Remember that you are in charge and what you believe goes, so consider whether you feel that the criticism is true or false. If false, ignore it and try not to waste any more time thinking about it. If it is true, or could be true, are you prepared to take ownership of it and to try to put it right? It is good if you are, but remember that it can take a while to change a lifetime habit, and there can be a period of time when things appear to get worse before they actually get better. In addition, just when you think you have mastered a new technique or attitude you can so easily slip back into your old ways once again – but if you can recognize it, then you have taken a step in the right direction.

❷ **Ask.** If you can't remember what your manager told you in your last appraisal, then take the bull by the horns and ask – either your boss, your colleagues or your subordinates. The best way to do this is not make it look too planned or prepared, otherwise people may feel threatened and will tell you what they think you want to hear rather than what they really think. Try to be casual and drop it into conversation; for example, take the opportunity when it arises and say something along the lines of, 'Oh, I am interested to hear you say that. It would help me to improve my performance if you could tell me whether that was all that was said', or, 'Could you give me a brief resumé of how my performance is perceived so that I can improve it in the future?'. It is rare for people to ask someone their opinion and they may therefore be taken aback, but on the whole people think good things about others and want to help them, so you may be pleasantly surprised by what is said!

If you really do want to hear what the person has to say, then you must help yourself and them by *listening*. It is all too tempting to jump in, defend yourself or finish off the person's sentence, but if you do this the opportunity will be lost for the person will lose their train of thought, clam up or wonder why you ever bothered to ask. Be brave, watch the person and wait for the answer. It may take a bit of time for them to gather their thoughts, but if you are patient the answer will come. Give it a try, for it is a powerful tool for gaining insight into your (widely known) trademark.

3 Become aware that others hold the answer. It is often easier to recognize faults in others than in yourself, so consider for a moment what you criticize other people for. Is it a certain type of behaviour, their attitude or their skills? If you recognize something to criticize in other people then it is likely to be a fault of your own as well, so look deep within yourself and try to take corrective action to put it right.

A good reputation needs a good trademark, so now is the time to change and to become an expert at what you do. Remember, though, that at any one time your trademark may or may not be based upon totally accurate information, so control it by regularly releasing positive snippets of information about your skills and performance to those around you.

DEVELOPING YOUR EXPERTISE

Anyone can do a job, but few people can do a job well. Now is your chance to become an asset to your organization by following the tips on how to develop your expertise given below.

✔ **Follow the rules.** Understand and follow the rules of the organization. Do what is required to fit in with the company structure and culture.

✔ **Take time to learn about the company and its people.** Read up about the company in its brochures and pamphlets and in the national press. Get a feel for who you are working for, what is important to the company, and how it is perceived locally, nationally and internationally. Observe and watch the people within the organization. Gain an insight into what motivates and drives them, for you need to make yourself look good without treading on other people's toes or making them look bad. Carry out as much research in this area as you can.

Having a good memory for facts, figures and people is vital and will work to your advantage if you use it correctly. I once sat next to someone at dinner who took great delight in re-telling a funny story: it was a pity that my guest had remembered all the facts but not the source of the tale, for the incident had happened to me and I had told the person the story last time we had met! So, be careful when you recount anything you have heard, as it could make you look a fool unless you remember *all* the facts.

✔ **Know your product.** It counts for a great deal if you understand what your company does or produces. If you don't already know, make it your business to find out about the product, its position in the market, its share of the market in monetary terms, its advantages and disadvantages, and the competition and its size. If you understand all this, then you will be able to relate to and understand the business as a whole. You will then be able to talk on the subject with conviction and knowledge.

✔ **Do your job.** Perform all of your job requirements, not just the glamorous or nice bits. Sometimes the little things in a job become the big issues, which can be blown out of all proportion. To avoid this, dig out a job description and check that you are fulfilling your duty to your employer. If not, take action immediately by either doing the extra bits yourself or finding ways to delegate but manage the tasks. Always pay attention to detail and ensure that you communicate what you do to your superior; otherwise, your boss could be judging you on totally different criteria, and this could give you a nasty shock at an appraisal. Ensure that such judgement is based upon factual information.

✔ **Be technical.** Technical knowledge is a real attribute, and vital if you want to be regarded as an expert. You need to understand all the ins and outs of the job better than anyone else. In addition, try to talk in terms of facts and figures rather than using vague concepts which often mean little and will be noticed by others.

✔ **Be committed.** Companies place great importance on
qualities such as commitment and loyalty. Know where your
loyalties lie, and if you do feel anything less than loyal keep
this information to yourself, or your company may leave
you out or pass you over. Watch your step and stress your
allegiance.

✔ **Enjoy what you do.** It is relatively easy to be good at
something if you enjoy it. In fact, work can be enjoyable,
fun and exciting rather than a drudge. You want to avoid
climbing up the career ladder only to discover when you get
to the top that it wasn't what you wanted after all, so ask
yourself whether this is really what you want to do. Put
your mind to performing well and giving your very best,
and you will do just that.

High-quality performance

Quality turns something ordinary into something exceptional. A
quality work performance is not just a requirement, but a necessity.
Such a performance:

✔ Fulfils the requirements.

✔ Satisfies the internal or external customer.

✔ Is long term rather than short term.

✔ Meets the deadline.

✔ Is right first time.

✔ Is presented accurately and professionally.

✔ Is in line with the specification.

✔ Is appreciated by the recipient.

People find it easier to do something well if they enjoy it. A contact
of mine is a very specialized teacher, and her professional reputation

is held in high esteem and demand. I asked her what was the secret of her success and she replied: 'I am in a responsible position and I owe it to myself, my profession and my tutors to provide equal, fair and effective teaching for all my pupils. My teaching is part of my heart – I just love it'. 'Quality' can be interpreted differently, but the overall message is to commit yourself to providing an efficient and effective service. The benefit to you is that quality increases motivation and energy and will lead to greater success.

THE PERFORMANCE APPRAISAL

The purpose of this exercise is to establish how good your performance is and to identify any areas in need of improvement. You know what you do well, what you find difficult or easy, and why something may or may not have been completed, so completing the appraisal should be relatively easy. Read through each section below and then tick the appropriate column to assess your performance.

Duties. A duty is what you are required to do in your job. Choose your five key duties and assess your performance of each one. Are you good at what you do, and have you been commended for carrying out the task? How quickly do you carry out the task, and would extra training be beneficial? One way of judging how good you are is to ask yourself whether or not you could teach someone else the duty.

	Duty	Below average	On par with colleagues	Excellent
1	_____	☐	☐	☐
2	_____	☐	☐	☐
3	_____	☐	☐	☐
4	_____	☐	☐	☐
5	_____	☐	☐	☐

Clients and contacts. The number of clients/contacts people have is a good performance indicator. What does your client/contact database look like? Does it consist mostly of old inherited clients or an equal mixture of old and new clients? Be honest with yourself and mark your performance accordingly.

	Below average	On par with colleagues	Excellent
Number of clients	☐	☐	☐

Relationship with the boss. How committed is your boss to you and your job? Do you regularly discuss your performance and future, or are you left to get on with the job by yourself? Is this an area for concern or improvement, or do you have a role model in your boss? Mark yourself on the basis of these questions.

	Below average	On par with colleagues	Excellent
Relationship with the boss	☐	☐	☐

Targets. Do you have clearly defined job targets for the next six months or year? Have you discussed these targets with your boss? Do you set easily achievable goals, or are you always striving for bigger and better things? Are you on line to achieve your current targets?

	Below average	On par with colleagues	Excellent
Targets	☐	☐	☐

The grapevine. What does the grapevine say about your performance? Do you hear complimentary things, nothing at all or, worse still, negative comments? Are you promoting yourself enough, or have you put yourself out to graze?

	Below average	On par with colleagues	Excellent
The grapevine	☐	☐	☐

Cross functioning. Do you mix and work across all functions? In fact, do people in other sectors even know who you are? Could you be more active in this area in order to increase your profile?

	Below average	On par with colleagues	Excellent
Cross functioning	☐	☐	☐

People. Are you a 'people person', seeing eye to eye with others, or are you constantly battling to be heard, seen or noticed? Do you need to calm down and recognize the value in others, seeing people as your allies rather than your enemies.

	Below average	On par with colleagues	Excellent
People	☐	☐	☐

At the end of this exercise you should have a clear idea of how you rate your performance. There are no marks for the appraisal because it is easy to see which areas need attention. Performance is not just about getting a job done: it is also about ensuring that you, the team and the division match up to the overall corporate goals.

Managing your time

Learning to manage your time is not easy: it involves having the confidence to do what you want to do and sticking to your plan despite external resistance. In order to manage your time, there are a number of things you need to do.

❶ Focus on what is important to you rather than how long it will take. Recognize what is driving you: what do you really want? For example, you may want to:

- Spend more time at home or travelling.

- Get fit.

- Get involved in extra-curricula activities.

- Be involved in certain projects at work.

- Make more off-site visits.

- Have greater flexibility of working hours.

❷ Focus on making a lifestyle change rather than changing something for a week or two. It takes courage to recognize and make a change, so you need to muster up as much support as you can. For example, many people when they get back from holiday decide that they are going to work fewer hours. However, they often fall back into their old ways as soon as a crisis occurs at work. They repeat all their old behaviours and then begin to feel resentful that they have no time to do the things they want to do. The reason it is so easy for people to be drawn back into their old habits is because they fail to make a lifestyle change, so there is nothing preventing them from slipping back into their old shoes.

What you actually need to do is to merge your paradigms together and adopt a less rigid view of time. For example, a client of mine wanted to spend more time at home and also to get fit. The way he achieved this was to join a leisure club where his family could also pursue leisure activities.

❸ Live in the present. Become absorbed with what you are doing in the here and now. The more you focus on the job in hand and what is required, the less you will worry about other issues and the easier it will be to complete the task.

❹ Focus on what you can do. Try to adopt a 'can do' approach to situations. Focus on what you are good at or what benefit you can bring. You need to believe in yourself and this will enable others to value you as well. Learn to spread good impressions about yourself.

⑤ Focus on what you want. Nobody else is going to do this for you, so if you want something it is up to you to achieve it. It is no good hoping or thinking that something will 'crop up' – instead take action to ensure that it does happen.

⑥ Resist the temptation to think about success or failure. Instead, commit yourself to the task and give it your best. Under these circumstances it is far more likely that it will be a success, because your enthusiasm will enlist the support of others.

Avoiding common pitfalls

The pitfalls are there for anyone to fall into. Your job is to avoid them like the plague, otherwise your reputation will be damaged. Listed below are the usual traps that people fall into *simply because they are unaware of them.*

An unpleasant manner. Perhaps you've been called cold, aggressive, or brusque? If this is the case, try to adopt a softer and more friendly approach.

The quickest and simplest way to do this is to smile. Smiling warms people to you and quickly breaks down barriers. If you can smile more – but be aware of grinning nervously – you will demonstrate that you are a confident person. This in turn will promote a positive image of yourself. Try it – you may be surprised at the response you receive!

Talking about previous jobs. Do you regularly talk about what you did in your previous job or compare what you do in your current company with what you did in other organizations for which you have worked? No one is actually disputing how brilliant you are, or what a good job you did in your previous company – remember that you don't have to prove yourself all the time. It is inadvisable to brag or to force other people to listen to your job or life history. What is past is past, and it is not particularly relevant to the present. In fact, talking about or reminding others of past conquests conveys a lack of self-confidence and self-belief, so that people might jump to conclusions and think that you are not performing in your current role. If a person *is* achieving in their current role, they tend to talk about the present rather than the past.

In order to be liked and accepted by others, let them discover your background gradually. Give people the satisfaction of telling you how certain things are done in your current organization; they will then warm to you and be much more willing to listen to your ideas. Share centre stage and let other people have their say as well.

Avoiding getting your hands dirty. Do you do your equal share of the less glamorous jobs, or are you inclined to delegate these to other people? Do you actually know what is required to do the task? If not, then find out. Accept that you cannot possibly know everything and there will always be times when you need to ask for help or to learn from other people.

Beware of avoiding certain tasks, because this does not go unnoticed. It sounds obvious, but you should get stuck in and do your share of the less appealing jobs, otherwise you will gain an unenviable reputation for not pulling your weight. Accept your share gracefully and you will soon gain a reputation as a doer.

Straying from the issue. Do you stray from the issue in hand by asking irrelevant, embarassing, ethical or sensitive questions about the company itself or about people's private lives?

It is not a good idea to ask any questions of this sort. Information gathering of this kind will almost certainly be regarded with suspicion, or could receive an angry response such as, 'Mind your own business'. Also it is easy to be drawn into conversations where you could reveal secrets about yourself which you would later regret, especially if they are spread around the office. Stick to questions which will help you to carry out your specified tasks; do not be afraid to ask basic questions, but make sure that when you ask a question in a group situation it is about the issue in hand, otherwise you will merely irritate your colleagues.

Not listening. Do you interrupt people when they are talking, or are you guilty of shifting the conversation on to other subjects?

Very few people actually listen to others – most simply wait until the person has stopped talking so that they can start. A failure to listen is not only bad manners but also a habit, so try to concentrate on what the speaker is saying. Keep all your questions until the end – there is a lot to learn in a job, but you will not be learning if you are doing all the talking. Realize also that you will find out much more if you are prepared to listen to other people.

A bad image. Are you a bit lax in the area of personal grooming (for example, hair, cleanliness, clothes and overall impression)?

Your image is important and reflects on you, your success and your personality. Good grooming is not dependent upon memory but upon care and attention; it does not mean having the best clothes, but ensuring that you look your best. People have good memories for things they don't like and it is often difficult to live down a loud tie, outrageous jewellery or a skimpy outfit. The general rules are as follows:

- **Clothes.** Choose clothes that reflect the company rather than your individuality, for what is special to you may not be to your organization. If in doubt, always dress conservatively to ensure that you don't slip up. Men should stick to dark suits, quality shoes, clean well-pressed shirts and suitable business ties. Women should choose suits or dresses rather than trousers, clean tailored shirts, quality lowish-heeled shoes and minimal jewellery.

- **Grooming.** Ensure that hair is clean, and regularly styled and cut. Remove any facial or nasal hair. Men should also ensure that they have a close shave once a day, and again in the evening if they have an appointment.

- **Accessories.** These are intended to complement an outfit, so ensure that all accessories such as pens, bags and briefcases are in good condition.

Flirtatious behaviour. Do you treat everyone the same, whether man or a woman, or do you use the office to seek your next date?

Most organizations have the partner hunters, who stalk out other people for personal relationships. Beware – you may be charmed and flattered by the attention and not realize that you are a target. Casanovas tend to make their conquests widely known, causing unnecessary embarrassment and even ruining a person's professional reputation. Steer clear of people of this kind, and wherever possible treat everyone in the same way.

Robbing the employer. Do you take more than your fair share from your employer?

The easiest way to 'rob' your employer is to take advantage of your privileges and use them for personal rather than business purposes. For example, a client of mine once told me that an employee of his had spent so long on the telephone to his family abroad that it would have been cheaper to buy him an air ticket to go and see them! These days, most extension numbers are logged and checked regularly, so don't kid yourself that a locked door or a quiet shift will ensure your anonymity. Go easy on the expense account as well, because senior managers notice how often, how much and how regularly their employees abuse the system. In short, try to avoid any behaviour which detracts from your being regarded as a hardworking, reliable, dedicated employee.

Unpredictable behaviour. Are you a reliable, predictable, responsible person? Or do you sneak off early, take extra-long breaks or lunch hours, or disappear for hours for no apparent reason?

Predictable behaviour is what is required, so fit in with the rules, don't try your luck and do what you promise, because someone, somewhere will be relying on you. Don't let yourself down by letting other people down. Show consideration for others by leaving contact telephone numbers whenever absent from the office, and ring if you have been unavailable for a while in order to collect any messages and to re-advise of your further movements. Conduct of this sort indicates that a person has nothing to hide and that he/she is doing their utmost to help others. Predictable behaviour therefore generates confidence in a person's abilities, attitude and intentions, so never underestimate the value of openness.

Not being a people person. Are you as interested in other people as you are in yourself? A 'people person' is someone who is genuinely interested in and caring towards others. It is a quality which tends to be in-built, but it can be learnt and practised. A people person:

✔ **Values others.** Everyone is unique and has their own special qualities and talents, so learn to recognize the good in others. Be interested in other people and they will be interested in you.

✔ **Understands others.** Recognize what motivates and drives other people, as it may not be the same as for you.

✔ **Doesn't take him/herself or others too seriously.** Inject an element of humour into situations or point out the funny side, as this will help to ease the pressure and strike a common chord with others.

✔ **Is trustworthy.** Discretion helps to form lasting relationships, so if someone tells you something in confidence keep it to yourself and their trust in you will grow.

✔ **Can wait his/her turn.** Accept the element of give and take. Let everyone have their share of the good, for there is plenty of it to go around.

✔ **Can share.** People who can share with others rather than hoarding clients, customers or good ideas have a greater support system when they need it than those who can't, won't or are unable to share.

✔ **Compliments others.** Do not underestimate the power of a sincere compliment. Few people receive them and even fewer give them, so try to give praise where it is due.

Forgetting things. Do you forget what you have been told, asked to do or even to attend certain appointments, meetings or functions?

A bad memory can haunt you if you don't manage it properly. It is not acceptable to forget in business because other people will remember, especially if it is a habit of yours. If you do forget something, the best policy is always honesty. Either ring up, write or go to see the relevant person and apologize. People rarely hold grudges against someone who has the guts to say 'sorry'. The next step is to take action, for it mustn't be allowed to happen again, so review your diary system or write yourself reminders.

Follow the guidelines in this chapter to become a specialist in your field – an expert who will be sought after by employers and targeted by headhunters in the future.

FOUR

Promoting Yourself

The business world wants to know about people's successes and expertise, so if you are proud of what you do, are an expert in your field of work or are doing particularly well, don't keep it a secret. Companies are constantly looking out for fresh talent to give them a competitive advantage and to take them forward: start to publicize what you have to offer and you will soon come to the attention of employers and headhunters.

This chapter will show you how to promote yourself in a businesslike manner without antagonizing, threatening or distancing yourself from others, in order to give yourself the best chance of being headhunted. The key self-promotion issues addressed here are:

- Networking.

- Giving a television interview.

- Giving a radio interview.

- Writing articles.

Self-promotion is crucial to your future success. You need to promote yourself to remind people of your existence and qualities. You must recognize that if you don't promote yourself you will start to lose ground and give other people an opportunity to overtake you in the race to be headhunted for the top jobs. To be successful it is necessary to master some, if not all, of the above self-promotion techniques. In addition, it will mean that you remain in charge of your career and avoid letting other people determine a less favourable future for you.

Networking

'It is not what you know, but who you know'. Business is about people – people who have the power to influence, decide and implement. The key is to focus on the importance of the people within your profession and to meet, mix and communicate with them. This includes *everyone*: it is important to treat each person with the same respect, whether they are higher up the scale or lower down the pecking order. Try to focus on making everyone around you feel important and special because they are.

Behaving in this way builds valuable and trustworthy relationships, and good relationships are the crux of a business. People prefer to do business with like-minded people, who have similar values, ideas and concepts to their own. For example, when making an appointment managers often tap into the 'network' and ask people what the grapevine has to say about a particular candidate in order to help them arrive at a decision. Thus, the way you manage your relationships has a direct bearing on your career development and progression, and you should therefore treat people in the same way as you would wish to be treated yourself. Remember, too, that it is never worth 'falling out' with people in business, because you never know when you might need them again!

The points listed below will help you consciously to develop a strong and supportive business network that will increase the chances of your being headhunted.

Walk the floor. Make people feel involved by going to see them, and keeping them up to date with the latest developments. Avoid falling into the trap of sitting in your office or meetings all day long or people will start to feel left out, excluded and isolated.

Keep in touch. Tell people what you are up to by writing, phoning or going to see them. Let past and present colleagues, past bosses, friends, agencies and contacts know about your job move, promotion, or latest career developments. Remember that no employer or headhunter will ever be able to find you if they don't know where to look, so keep people informed.

Congratulate people. Remember how wonderful it is to receive a compliment? Well, start to give a few and then you may receive even more. Be happy for and proud of other people's successes and achievements, as well as your own. For example, when you read about a contact's accomplishments and new job, or if they appear in the press, write to congratulate them. People appreciate recognition, so give it a try. Most won't bother to do it, but if you do your friends will remember you for it. An example of a congratulatory letter is given below.

Dear _____

Congratulations on your new appointment to _____ which I read about in_____. I am pleased to see that you are staying in London and will contact you soon to meet up.

Keep up the good work.

Regards

_____

Be interested in people. Look at people and listen to what they are saying, rather than looking over their shoulder to find someone different to talk to, interrupting, or waiting for the person to finish talking so that you can start again. Build upon what has already been said and look genuinely interested in what the speaker is saying. Don't fall into the trap of thinking you should do all the talking: communication is a two-way process and other people like to talk as well.

Try to develop your memory for names and faces. A good way to do this is to exchange business cards and to write some notes on the back. The next time you ring the person you can refer to your previous conversation – and probably even remember what they look like! Make it your business to remember and be interested in others, as it will do wonders for your reputation.

Give thanks. Another way to show your appreciation is to say 'thank you' to people who have done something for you, whether it be a friend, a contact, a journalist or a colleague. Thanking people bonds you together and is a genuine acknowledgement of your gratitude.

Help people. If you can help someone, then do it. Perhaps you can set up a meeting, recommend someone, or make an initial introduction on their behalf – whatever it is, take the time and opportunity to do things for others, for in some situations it is possible to help people more than they can help themselves. And wouldn't you want them to do the same for you some time?

Be visible. Part of building and promoting a reputation is about putting yourself in the public eye. Create opportunities for yourself to be seen and noticed, and these will help you to be picked out and then selected by employers. You can network anywhere, but read the list below to see if you can increase your networking possibilities.

✔ Join professional clubs, institutions or work-related associations.

✔ Follow up contacts you have in the profession. Write to or ring them in order to get back on terms again.

✔ Network with people you work with during lunch hours or after work.

✔ Go to functions you have been invited to.

✔ Get yourself on the mailing lists of professional magazines so that you can find out what is going on and where.

✔ Call in on your contacts if you are in the vicinity or driving past. Make people feel that they are important to you and they will then reciprocate. Share information and help each other.

✔ Be accessible and available to friends and colleagues. Try to agree mutually convenient arrangements.

✔ Contact your college or university and update them on your career to date. Attend and support their functions and activities, and establish new relationships at these events. Draw upon the college's sources of information about companies and key people in those organizations, who you may need to meet in order to support your career.

The networking list is almost endless, but good networkers will know people involved in key operations and be able to create opportunities for themselves when they need them. They will use contacts to their advantage, or their reputation in the profession will open the necessary doors. Make sure you value the power of networking and use every avenue to increase your visibility.

Speak in public. Speaking, lecturing or presenting in public is a necessity if you want to boost your visibility and profile, and once you start the invitations to do more will flood in. To gain confidence, start on a small scale and build up your experience gradually. Offer to do a talk on your key subjects at work, and at your local committee or institution meetings. Keep your presentations simple and fairly short. Where possible use overheads, slides or props, as this helps to keep the audience alert and interested.

In addition, promote yourself by writing to the local or national radio stations and television channels, explaining how they could benefit from your areas of expertise. The example opposite of a letter written by a travel consultant who did this should give you plenty of ideas.

The next step is to do what you have promised. Letters of this kind can generate opportunities for you, and if you get a chance to appear on the radio don't forget to write and thank the person who made it all possible.

It is hard work to network and keep in touch with people, but if you can you will build a strong and supportive group of contacts around you whom you can call on when you need to create career opportunities for yourself. The key is to recognize the importance of networking and to keep at it all the time.

Home address

Date

Name

Address

Dear _____

I have been listening to the exciting issues you are covering on Radio _____ at the moment. [*State your interest in the programme.*] There is no doubt that you present new ideas, new angles and up-to-date issues in order to keep the listener's interest alive. [*Compliment the organization.*]

How would you feel about doing a weekly 'travel spot' related to popular destinations, late bargains and traveller tips? I am sure it would be a popular and desirable topic for your listeners at this time of year. [*State your proposal and suggest ideas.*] You might want to consider aspects such as:

1 The travel market. How people travel at different times of year and the most popular destinations. Who can offer what. The average amount of money spent per person on a holiday.

2 Traveller tips. How to prepare for your holiday in terms of money, vaccinations, and health and travel insurance. What to do in case of a delay or claim.

3 The latest bargains. What bargains are around each week on a range of holidays. How to look for a bargain holiday.

I am a professional travel consultant [*List qualifications here.*] who has 20 years' experience in the business. I have many contacts and resources to draw upon in offering you this service.

I would be grateful if we could meet up to discuss the proposal and for me to hear your ideas on the subject as well. I will contact you at the end of the week so that we can arrange a mutually convenient time.

Yours faithfully

_____

Television interviews

The more successful and widely known you become, the greater your chances of being invited to make a guest appearance to speak on television. Most people feel daunted by this prospect, particularly if they have never done it before: the stakes are high and no one wants to make themselves look a fool, fail to get their point across or make a mistake. However, if you do your homework beforehand you are unlikely to slip up.

Television is a highly specialized and powerful medium. Most people are not natural television presenters and have to learn how to come across well, present themselves and put over their message. A good performance will give you enormous satisfaction and pleasure, as well as boosting your career by winning public credibility and recognition.

PREPARATION

In order to give a good performance, you need to prepare every detail before setting foot in the television studio. A list of things to consider is given below.

- **The programme.** Will you be appearing on a formal show, a chat show or a news programme? You need to establish the style, format and tone of the show, so try to watch the programme beforehand to enable you to pitch your presentation accordingly.

- **The time.** How long will you be on the air? Establish this beforehand so that you can carry out adequate preparation. In addition to the length of the interview, you also need to know what time you need to be at the studio in order to rehearse and have your make-up done. (Make-up is vital for you to look your best; make-up artists can cover up any blemishes or skin-colour problems, conceal dark circles under the eyes or deep lines, and make the difference between looking ordinary and well-groomed.)

- **Alone or in company?** Establish whether you will be appearing on the show alone or with others, as this will affect your time allocation and the tone of the interview. For example, it is usual for both sides of an argument to be presented and they will be allotted equal time. However, if you are to appear on your own, be prepared for the interviewer to take up the opposite viewpoint to yours in order to present a balanced argument for the viewers at home. You will need to take account of this in your preparation.

- **The interviewer.** Watch the programme in advance so that you are familiar with the interviewer and his/her manner and style of questioning.

- **The location.** Make sure you know where the interview will take place – it is not unheard of for people to lose their television slot because they failed to turn up on time. Also ensure that you are shown in advance where to sit and how to use any equipment. If you are comfortable with the technicalities it is much easier to focus all your attention on the interview, the interviewer and your message.

YOUR MESSAGE

Time is of the essence in television, so make sure that your message is simple, appropriate and effective. To avoid running out of time or being cut off in mid-sentence, practice delivering your statement aloud beforehand. Focus on what you want to say and keep your message short: if it is too long, too detailed or too technical the salient points can be lost. It is far more important to communicate a few key issues than the whole long, drawn-out story, and it is always worth keeping a bit in reserve so that you can be invited back again!

You may be asked to appear on television in order to answer for something you may or may not have done or said. The key in these circumstances is to take your time, listening to all the 'allegations' against you rather than jumping in to defend yourself. Always take ownership of what you have done rather than trying to pass the buck or blame someone else, as this could lead to a hostile, ineffective interview where you are depicted in a bad light or, worse still, drawn into an argument. Defuse the situation by 'owning' the problem, presenting possible solutions and remaining positive throughout the interview. Try to avoid being defensive, turning unpleasant or making similar accusations yourself. Behaviour of this sort will not reflect well on you and will make you appear guilty even if you are not. Try to remain relaxed and calm, and remember to hold your ground.

PRACTICE

The key to a successful performance is practice, so try to create an opportunity for a mock television interview. It is worthwhile videoing it so that you can watch it afterwards and judge your own performance. Allow the same amount of time as allocated to the real interview and get your colleagues or someone you trust to ask you some tough questions. Gain feedback from your colleagues and then watch the interview yourself. How did you feel you came across? Undoubtedly, you can improve, and the guidelines below will help you to perfect your performance.

- **Look approachable.** Try to look friendly, open and relaxed rather than stiff and starchy. People who aren't approachable generally tend to take things and themselves too seriously, and in doing so can cause others to withdraw from them, even though these are the very people they want to impress!

  Appear approachable in how you sit, your gestures, and your facial expressions. Sit at the front of the seat rather than at the back to avoid slumping or disappearing into the sofa. As far as gestures are concerned, do what is natural for you. For example, if you use your hands a lot, then continue to do so, as doing what you are used to will help you to relax. The two main things to remember are to look the interviewer in the eye and to adopt a relaxed rather than a defensive posture (the latter involves crossing your arms and/or legs, or pointing your finger at the interviewer). Facial expressions are also important, so try to smile from time to time to help portray a positive image of yourself.

- **Strike up a rapport with the interviewer.** The interviewer wants the interview to be as successful as you do. He/she may also be just as nervous as you are, especially if it is a first-time interview. Try to develop common subjects and points of interest, and build upon what the interviewer has already said. Above all, remember that you are the expert in the subject and that is why you have been invited on to the show; recognize that you have something important to say which other people want to hear. Try to regard the interviewer as an ally rather than someone to feel frightened of or threatened by, for if you are at ease with yourself you will be much easier to interview, and the end result will be far better.

- **Consider your clothes.** The most important thing is to wear something which is comfortable. How many times have you seen people on television wearing a new outfit in which it is quite obvious that they are unable to walk properly? The rules for choosing clothes are simple: avoid wearing anything too bright, dark or light in colour, anything patterned or striped, or anything too revealing. In fact, avoid anything which will distract the viewer's attention from what you are saying! Choose instead traditional, plain clothes that suit you, preferably with pastel colours for your shirt or blouse. Where possible avoid white as it is affected by the bright lights and can cause you to look drained. For interviews conducted outside, choose clothes suitable for the weather. Having said all this, try not to get too worked up about your clothes, because the viewers probably won't see all that much of them anyway.

- **Consider your hair.** Your hair is important because it will be highly visible. It should therefore be neat, trim and well styled. It is also a good idea to use a bit of gel to ensure that your hair stays in place – especially if you are being filmed outside.

Radio interviews

Preparation for a radio interview is the same as that for a television interview, with the single addition of voice preparation. With radio, the audience doesn't have the advantage of seeing the speaker and so the voice and its quality is far more important. However, there is a fine balance between overdoing the emphasis so that you sound as if you are doing an elocution examination, and paying no attention to the voice so that it sounds flat, boring and uninteresting. Listed below are a few key points to help you to strike the right balance.

Pace is important. It is determined by the nature of the subject (for example, factual or technical subjects need a slower delivery than lighthearted, casual subjects), as well as by the capabilities of the speaker. Some people naturally talk much more quickly than others, but you must remember never to speak so quickly that the listener is unable to take it all in and will therefore switch off.

Pitch refers to the height or depth of the voice. Roughly speaking, there are three pitches: high, middle and low. Pitch is changed during a delivery to:

● Change the emotion. A high pitch is used for excitement or happiness, while sorrow is portrayed with a lower pitch. A medium pitch is normally used for subjects lacking emotion.

● Change the subject. A change of pitch in this instance ensures that the audience picks up the fact that the emphasis or subject matter has changed.

● Avoid monotony. A change of pitch helps to keep the audience's interest in a subject alive.

Inflection is the gentle rise and fall of the voice on the syllables of a passage within the pitch. For example, it is possible to use a falling inflection within a high pitch and a rising inflection within a low pitch, but not change the overall pitch. Inflection is used for a specific emphasis on a few words in order to bring these to the audience's attention. It is an individual and personal interpretation of the words spoken.

Tone is really the intensity of the voice: how loud or quiet, hard or soft, sympathetic or unsympathetic it is. How much tone you wish to portray is dependent upon the subject matter.

Pauses have a very important place, especially when you are speaking on the radio, as you have to give the audience time to absorb, understand and reflect upon what has been said. Don't therefore be tempted to race like a train from topic to topic, without pausing for breath. Pauses are also important for:

- Sense. When speaking, follow the same rules as for the written word and pause where you would for punctuation.

- Effect. A pause can make a word, phrase or sentence stand out, or it can help build up a climax. You can pause either before or after the section you want to emphasize.

Remember, too, that pausing demonstrates confidence, because you are at ease with what you are saying.

Being on the radio sometimes means talking via the telephone rather than sitting in a studio with the presenter. Under these circumstances your voice is all the more important, because not even the presenter can see you and gauge what you are like.

If you do not feel that your voice has many of the above-mentioned qualities, but appearing on radio will be a regular occurrence for you, then consider getting some professional help with your voice. A well-trained voice is a major asset, because it will increase your ability to command and hold an audience's attention.

Writing articles

Writing articles is the easiest way to become recognized publicly as an expert within your profession. Employers, and particularly headhunters, read newspapers, magazines and journals and they notice who is being mentioned or quoted, or is writing material themselves.

Most people don't submit written work to the press because they regard writing as something very special which requires skills they don't possess. However, this is not true: anyone who can talk about something with clarity, expression and interest can learn how to put their thoughts and ideas down on paper.

If you want to give your career a boost, then give article writing a try. This section will show you what to consider in order to write in a professional way which will increase the chances of your work being accepted and ultimately published.

HOW TO WRITE AN ARTICLE

The biggest mistake most people make is in *how* they write their article rather than *what* they write about. They may have any idea for a topic, write about it, and then try to get it published, but this is not the best policy because their approach and style, plus the angle of the subject matter, may not be what the editor is looking for in order to satisfy, entertain or educate his readers. The key is always to contact the editor before you put pen to paper, otherwise your time and effort are likely to be wasted. Unless something is tailored towards the intended publication there is a high chance of it being rejected, and although rejection is part of the agonies of writing in general and professional writers accept this as par for the course, for the novice rejection hits home hard and can put you off writing anything ever again. However, rejection can be avoided if you adopt the right attitude and follow the principles set out in the following sections to help you write, tailor and market your article.

The right attitude to writing means committing yourself to the task and seeing the project through. Recognize that if you have a good idea for an article, then others could benefit too by reading about it. However, remember also that magazines and newspapers are governed to some extent by their budgets, by what has previously been featured and what is already planned for the future. A 'no' answer from one publication may therefore be a 'yes' from another, so although getting published may not be all that easy it is *possible*. The key is to keep trying, and eventually you will reap the benefits of having a higher and more visible profile.

The market

The magazine and newspaper market is enormous, with literally thousands being published regularly on a huge range of subjects. Many of the well-known national publications have their own editorial people who are employed full-time to write the required material, but the smaller magazines, local newspapers and specialized journals tend to rely more heavily on freelance writers and/or submissions from readers. The key is to pick your publications carefully in order to avoid disappointment. It is far better to focus on smaller or professional publications or magazines initially, rather than diving in and contacting the big national ones. Once you have gained a name for yourself or are writing regularly for a local publication, you will be a much more attractive proposition for the nationals. In fact, they may even commission you to write something for them.

Principles of article writing

The principles of successful article writing are explained below. Follow these and it is unlikely to be long before you will see your work in print.

Think of an idea

The first step is to think of something to write about. The best idea is to write about what you know, are good at or have had personal experience of. You are an expert in something if you know much more about the subject than other people, so think about this in relation to your job and work. What do you do and what could you write about? Try to brainstorm lots of ideas rather than coming up with just one or two; when you phone the editor, it is worth presenting several options for him/her to choose from rather than just one, because the conversation will come to an abrupt end if the answer is 'No'! Think along the lines of:

- **Your technical expertise.** For example, the benefits of a particular qualification, the advantages of using certain procedures, or how training improved your performance.

- **Your company background.** For example, the difference between working for a multi-national company and a partnership or family-run business.

- **A day in the life of.** Aspiring recruits like to understand and appreciate what certain jobs and professions are about, so an article of this kind is a good starter – as are accounts of how someone got to the top and what qualities they value or have acquired along the way.

- **Personal experiences.** Most people have some interesting work experience to write about, and writing from experience helps you to speak with conviction and authority. You will also find that you can write better if the topic is something personal. Consider such areas as working abroad; time management; the changing face of your profession; travelling on business; or how to build up relationships and business with overseas customers.

- **The very latest equipment or procedures.** You may have the benefit of using or having access to the most up to date equipment or computer packages. If so, write about it – as other people are waiting to hear whether it is all it is cracked up to be!

Ideas generate other ideas, so have a go and see what you can come up with. Ideas are all around you in the workplace; the important thing is to be receptive to them and then your thoughts will start to flow, so keep your eyes open and listen to what people around you are talking about. Also have a look at the latest newspapers and magazine issues – what are they featuring? You can always use the same topic but write about it from a different or more personal angle. The key is to be creative and turn an everyday, normal work subject into something which you can write about.

Do your research

The next step is to research your target publication. Remember that it is never advisable to ring or contact an editor before you know a little about:

- The type of people reading the publication.

- What the readership look for from the publication.

- The editorial requirements.

If you do the necessary research you will be able to talk with knowledge and fulfil the editor's need, rather than appearing as if you are merely looking for an opportunity to plug your name and your expertise (neither of which an editor will mind, of course, as long as his readers get what they want as well).

Firstly, you need to establish who reads the target publication. Are they mainly men or women? Are they young, middle-aged or more senior? Are they affluent or not so well off? To help you answer these questions, look at the:

- **Publication's face.** What kind of person is depicted in its advertising or on the front cover?

- **Subject matter.** What sort of material does it contain? Are the issues covered technical, lighthearted or theoretical?

- **Advertising.** Advertisers don't like to waste money, so they research their readership and audience thoroughly. If, for example, the magazine carries advertisements for prestigious products, then the readership is likely to be affluent, while if the advertisements are for training or development courses, then the readership is likely to be technical and knowledgeable.

Understanding the lifestyle and attitude of the readers of your target publication is also important. Lifestyle is usually indicated by the age of the readership; for example, older people tend to be less mobile, spend less on disposable items and are less physically active than younger people, but have more money to spend.

In order to target and pitch the tone of your writing, you need to appreciate the readers' attitudes and outlook on life as well. Read your target publication and ask yourself:

- Is the readership made up of serious, thoughtful people who take an interest in business and the acquisition of knowledge, or are they looking for a lighthearted read?

- Does the readership have a traditional or modern outlook on life?

The next thing you need to establish is why people read your targeted publication and what they hope to get out of it. This can be categorised into three basic areas:

- **News** is usually based upon factual information to enable people to understand what is happening in a given situation and how it affects them personally. The reader can therefore learn how to do something better.

- **Information** is not the same as news. Here, the reader is informed about a situation in order that they can under-stand what to see, find or expect in these circumstances.

- **Entertainment** tends to apply to consumer magazines rather than trade or business publications.

Finally, you need to research the editorial requirements of your targeted publication. Much of this you will be able to clarify with the editor when you speak or write to him/her, but you can do some preparation beforehand. Consider:

- **Angle.** This is vitally important: you need to establish what approach is appropriate for your target publication and what angles haven't yet been covered. Over the years, most magazines will have covered many of the key subjects, but what makes material new, exciting and interesting is the angle the author takes. Time management, say, is a popular issue for business magazines, but if you approached an editor with this as your possible topic he/she would probably want the article written from a more unusual angle; for example, instead of writing about 'How to manage your time effectively', you could choose something along the lines of 'How to work fewer hours instead of more' or 'How to earn more money but work fewer hours'. Try to look at all the possible angles on a particular subject in order to make it up to date and therefore saleable.

Some editors prefer people to contact them by phone so that they can discuss the proposed article in depth, whereas others prefer you to write and send a synopsis or outline of the suggested material. The best policy is to try to phone first; speak to the editor and find out what his/her requirements are. The key is to sound authoritative and an expert in your subject, rather than saying that you have never done this before! Create interest in yourself and be enthusiastic about your idea – if you can come across as having something interesting to offer the magazine, then the editor will probably be interested in what you have to say.

Initially, introduce yourself and give the editor a brief resumé of your area of expertise and work background. Explain that you have an idea for an article: this is the point at which all your research will come into play. Perhaps you have an idea based upon something which has already been featured in the publication but your article would present another angle; alternatively, your idea may be based upon a personal experience or technical information. Try not to have too fixed an opinion on the subject matter and angle, because the editor has the final say and may want to change things slightly. Remember, too, that if an editor expresses interest in your idea and asks you to send in the article this doesn't guarantee that it will be published – the article may not be written in the correct style or format, it may not be in line with the original brief, or the editor may simply have changed his/her mind about the whole idea.

- **Word count.** Have a look at the articles carried in the magazine. Are they long, covering perhaps two pages, or are they short, covering just a few columns? Avoid wasting your time by writing something that is either too long or too short – always check with the editor on the preferred length for an article.

- **Vocabulary.** Study your target publication and note the choice of words. Are they simple and ordinary, or more technical and theoretical? Ensure that your article is written in a consistent style and avoid writing to impress, as it rarely has the desired effect.

- **Sentence and paragraph length.** Some publications carry long sentences and lengthy paragraphs whereas others prefer a shorter, snappier approach. Have a look at the publication and check out the style, then tailor your writing to your findings.

- **Visual appearance.** Note how the text appears on the page. It is unusual for an article to be printed as pure unbroken text: normally, it is broken up with headings, subheadings, pictures and graphs or other features. Try to follow what the publication already uses.

- **House style.** House style refers to the written standards that the publication follows. Typical house styles refer to the way numbers, dates and abbreviations are presented in the text; for example, the house style may be to write numbers up to ten in words and after ten in numbers, and/or to avoid abbreviations. If something isn't written in the house style it stands out like a sore thumb, so go through the publication in detail and note how the text is presented. Some magazines even publish guidelines on what they expect from their writers in terms of house style, and it is worth contacting the editorial office to see whether this is the case as it will save you work in the long run.

Once you have done all your research and embarked upon the writing, make sure you minimize the chances of rejection by delivering what the editor has asked for. Make their job easier by fulfilling the requested requirements, writing the article in the house style and delivering it on time. Then, never be afraid to ring up afterwards to find out how your article has been received or whether it needs changing slightly. Your aim is to see it finally in print!

Having read through this chapter, you will now realize that creating and promoting a reputation takes time and effort. You can't rush the process – it doesn't work that way, and people will see through this approach. The key is to take your time. More importantly than what you do, is to do what you *want* to do, for ultimately most people are looking for a long and fulfilling career rather than a successful but unfulfilled one. There is little point striving for years to get wherever it is, only to find that it is not where you wanted to be after all. The reverse is also true: you have a far greater chance of being successful and highly sought after if you find your work fulfilling. So, if you are fulfilled in your job, success is par for the course.

FIVE

Attitude, Appearance and Fitness

Your attitude, appearance and physical well-being are important in advancing your career and increasing your potential for being headhunted.

Attitude

Attitude is crucial as far as your career is concerned. It consists of the way you view yourself and your work, and how you interact with the people around you. Attitude is therefore picked up and interpreted by other people and, more importantly, affects the way others respond to you. In business, people are valued not purely in terms of what they produce but also for how they approach and deal with other people; those who have the right kind of attitude tend to be more productive and popular than those who pay little or no attention to their attitude. Listed below are a few tips to help you build your self-confidence by focusing on your attitude.

- **Look for the good.** Recognize that no one is perfect but that everyone has good qualities. People are trying to give their best in any situation, so focus on the good in others and talk about their positive attributes.

- **Be human.** Allow others to get to know you as a person, as it is very easy for people to get the wrong impression or to interpret things wrongly if they don't really understand you. Recognize that it is far better for you to communicate the truth than for others to make things up.

- **Build relationships with everyone.** Relationships are based on mutual trust, information and communication. Concentrate on building equal relationships with everyone including your peers, colleagues, subordinates, boss and superiors. Spending more time on some relationships than others could be dangerous, as other people can feel left out or threatened and will then act accordingly.

  Recognize also that there is a grapevine and that people talk, so avoid feeding the grapevine and creating problems in your relationships by being thoughtless and tactless. For example, avoid criticizing people to others as it will only reflect back on you if these comments are passed on. Be careful what you say about others and don't spoil your relationships.

- **Understand other people.** Try to avoid jumping to conclusions, reacting instantly to situations or reading things into them. Instead, try to put yourself in the other person's shoes and understand why they said something or behaved in a certain way. To do this, concentrate on the facts and detach yourself from the emotion of the situation. You can then overcome the barriers by showing empathy and trying to understand what is motivating or driving the other person to behave in the way that they are. Once you have achieved this, you will be better able to accept people for who they are rather than wanting them to be someone different.

- **Be open.** Try to be open and sensitive to the needs of others, as well as to change within your environment. Adapt or modify your attitude in accordance with the situation and stay flexible, as this will help you to reduce any pressure or stress and to live in the present.

- **Hold on to your positive attitude.** Maintaining a positive attitude is difficult, but if you can things will be brighter for you and people will want you around them. Protect your attitude by refusing to allow other people's negative attitudes to cloud your perception or spoil things for you.

Appearance and exercise

A career is similar to a long-distance race. It requires energy, stamina and fitness in order to work long hours and meet heavy schedules, and if you want to do well and to stay in the 'race' long term then you will need to exercise regularly. Exercise helps you to keep fit, to unwind and to stay in top form. It also improves your appearance – and in the world of work prejudice against those in poor physical shape can have an adverse effect on their career. Above all, exercise should be fun and will make you feel good as well as do you some good! The key is not to rush at it or overdo it, but to start by doing gentle exercise and build it up gradually – train but don't strain.

When you decide to start exercising, it is important to try to take up a sport which you enjoy, otherwise you are likely to do it once or twice and give it up – and then probably feel guilty about it. When making your choice, pick something which is feasible and accessible: for example, a client of mine's main sporting interest was tennis, but he only seemed to play once in a blue moon because it was difficult for him to find people of an equal or better standard than himself to play against. As joining a tennis club with all-year-round facilities wasn't an option, he decided to pursue other activities but still enjoyed the occasional game of tennis. The best option is to choose a sport which fits into your daily or weekly routine and which isn't too heavily dependent upon other people for their participation or support.

If you are looking for the optimum results from your exercise efforts and a transformed body, then you will need to strike a balance between aerobic and anaerobic activities. Aerobic exercise includes such things as jogging, cycling, swimming or fitness classes, while anaerobic work includes muscle strengthening and toning by training with weights. Many people are happy to design a fitness programme for themselves, whereas others prefer to attend a private or council-run health and leisure club where experts will design and monitor your fitness programme to ensure the best results. You can also take the opportunity to keep fit by being active throughout the day by walking or climbing stairs rather than using the car, lift or escalator. The important thing with exercise is to be safe, and if you are in any doubt always seek professional medical advice. Listed below are a few tips to ensure productive, safe and effective exercise:

- **Have a medical check up.** Before starting to exercise and perhaps taking unnecessary risks, get your doctor to check you out, especially if you have a medical condition or haven't exercised for a long time.

- **Don't overdo it.** Be conscious of how you feel and perform when you exercise. If you feel tired or any pain, then stop. Stretch your muscles and rest. Avoid pushing yourself too far too fast, and build up your stamina and strength slowly. It will pay off in the long run.

- **Warm up and then exercise.** Always warm up your body before you exercise. Stretching muscles before you start to exercise reduces the risk of injury or stiffness.

- **Have a cooling-down period.** After exercising, cool down by stretching muscles and then gently shaking each arm and leg in turn.

- **Rest and relax.** Refresh yourself with a bath, shower, jacuzzi, or a sauna. Take the time to refresh yourself and rest your body after exercise.

- **Exercise and then eat.** For safety and hygiene reasons, don't eat or chew gum while exercising. Leave about two hours between eating and exercising in order to avoid stomach cramps or discomfort.

- **Pay attention to your clothes.** Choose and wear appropriate footwear and loose-fitting clothing (many injuries are caused because people fail to select the right kind of footwear). If it is cold, wear extra clothing to prevent cramps. If you exercise at a sports club, be extra careful about what you wear because not adhering to the proper dress codes can offend others.

- **Don't exercise if you are unwell.** Avoid exercising if you feel unwell or under the weather, as this will affect your performance and could make you feel even worse afterwards.

● **Avoid exercising in the heat of the day.** You can dehydrate very quickly in hot weather, so try to exercise when the temperature is cooler.

● **Keep at it.** To ensure the best results and a long-term benefit, you need to keep exercising. Before long you may find that exercising becomes an essential part of your life, because not only does it make you feel better, but it gives you more energy, increases your ability to concentrate, makes you sleep better and helps you to dissolve stress more quickly. In fact, the benefits far outweigh the effort required to do it!

Watching your weight

Your weight is important, because whether you like it or not people are affected by the way you look. There is prejudice against people who are over- or underweight; those who are classed as being over weight are often mistakenly regarded lazy, unhealthy or lacking self-discipline, while people who are underweight are often seen as being mean or having psychological problems. You need to recognize that your size or weight may be causing others to discriminate against you in terms of career advancement.

A healthy person is someone who is the right weight for his/her height and bone structure. It is impossible to be specific about dietary levels because people have different requirements according to their age, build, activity level, height and sex. The key is to watch what you eat and to be happy with how you look, and if you honestly can't maintain the right sort of weight then consider seeing a dietician. In the meantime, do what you can with your clothes in order to disguise your size and keep exercising.

SIX

Headhunting Procedures

Headhunters are specialists in recruitment. They have detailed technical knowledge of their field or fields and they know where to find the key people who are good at what they do and have a worthy reputation. Even more important than knowing where to find these people, the headhunter has direct access to them to talk about new career initiatives.

It is because of this level of expertise that employers turn to headhunters when they have specific recruitment requirements. The headhunter works on behalf of the employer to manage the whole recruitment process from initial introduction to final appointment. He/she identifies, approaches and puts forward suitable and interested candidates to the employer, then manages the process and advises both the successful and unsuccessful candidates of the employer's decision.

The headhunter's role is complex and important, and requires a lot of research, patience and experience in order to ensure that the best possible person is found and appointed.

Why use a headhunter?

Employers choose to use a headhunter when they have a specific job or position to fill which requires a certain type of person, level of experience and particular knowledge. If the employer is not in a position to appoint someone from within the organization he/she has to look at the external possibilities. Advertising this post in the local, national or technical press may not have produced a suitable response, or the employer may know from experience that advertising the job will not generate the right sort of replies. The reason for this is that specialist jobs require special people to perform them, and although there may not be a shortage of people with the right capabilities, skills and experience, those with the appropriate background may not be on the job market. Usually these people are in work and are well regarded by their current employer but are not currently looking for new work so placing an advertisement will have little effect. However, these people may possibly be dissatisfied, unfulfilled, blocked, or needing something extra special, and this is where headhunters come into their own, for they can research the whole potential market, and track down and highlight the right kind of person for the employer. Employers may invite several headhunters to talk to them about the quality and range of their service, their expertise in the given field, and their terms and conditions in order to make their choice, or the employer may choose a suitable headhunter on the basis of a recommendation from a contact or client.

The service provided by headhunters is individual, personal, sensitive and confidential, and is tailored to suit the needs, demands and specifications of the employer. Quality service of this kind is expensive, with the normal rates being 30–35 per cent of the appointed person's salary. Generally, one-third of the fee is paid when the headhunter is awarded the assignment, one-third when the headhunter submits the shortlist of candidates to the employer, and the remaining one-third when the person joins the company. Most headhunters also offer some form of refund or a second chance to find someone else at no extra cost in the event of the appointee being unsuitable or leaving within three to six months of joining the organization. The exact terms and conditions will be laid out in the headhunter's contract. In terms of evaluating the cost, one of my clients commented that 'There is no denying that appointing a headhunter is an expensive method of recruitment, but for key positions the organization feels it is worthwhile. The headhunters we use have a team of researchers who consider all the possibilities and key areas in order to find people on our behalf. They know their stuff, but more importantly they come up with the goods'.

Preparing the specification

Once the headhunter has been appointed, the employer and headhunter will work through the detailed specification of the job and the preferred criteria for selection of candidates. The original specification will be fleshed out to incorporate details such as the culture of the organization; age of the applicant; personality attributes; level of experience; qualifications; managerial qualities; exact job title, responsibilities and position within the organization; salary and benefits; relocation package; and terms and conditions.

The next step is for the employer to direct the headhunter as to where to look. Headhunters have their own contacts and clients within their fields, but employers can usually provide additional information such as the types of organizations the people they want to employ will be working for, while some might even go so far as indicating the names of prospective candidates. The more specific and accurate an employer can be, the easier it will be for the headhunter to pinpoint and select the right people.

Finding the right person

Headhunters work on specific assignments for their clients, so you are only likely to hear from one headhunter when he/she has a position to fill. Headhunters do not need to store information on a database or hold CVs on file, because they can find people when they need to.

Headhunters work to tight schedules, because although employers are usually prepared to wait a while for the right person to be found, they will not hang on forever. The usual timescale is six to eight weeks from awarding the headhunting contract to the shortlisted stage. This gives the headhunter approximately four weeks to do all the necessary research and the remaining two weeks to screen all the applicants by initial interviews and carry out any necessary procedures such as personality tests.

After six weeks' work, the headhunter is usually in a position to advise the client of all the suitable shortlisted candidates. He/she will put forward a handful of candidates to the employer, all of whom meet the original specification. A detailed report is supplied on each candidate covering their abilities, experience, company background and education, and sometimes a personality profile is included as well. In addition, the headhunter will usually add their personal opinion of each person put forward.

At this point the headhunter hands over the candidates to the employer, who carries out the next stage of interviews. However, the headhunter is in regular contact with the employer to check on progress and to arrange the interview dates and times. Finally, the employer advises the headhunter on the successful candidate and the headhunter then relays the good or bad news, and negotiates and co-ordinates notice periods where necessary.

So, how do headhunters find people? A headhunter's greatest asset is their research team, who actually make the phone calls and tap into the network of an organization. The members of this team are specialists in the field of work and they know all the contacts within the business. Every headhunting organization has its own particular procedures, practices and 'tricks of the trade', which they will keep secret if they want to maintain their position in the market. However, some typical procedures used by headhunters in order to home in on key business people are described below.

CONTACTING COMPANIES

Headhunters are likely to talk to every company in the same field of business as the client who instructed them. The reason for this is that the headhunter is compiling lists of the best candidates, and there is no guarantee as to where these people will be. Headhunters therefore search far and wide, but also deep.

When the headhunter contacts an organization he/she may talk to one of the directors, the head of the department, or a personal contact. Initially, the headhunter is after general information in order to establish who might or might not be a suitable candidate for the position, and if you received a call of this nature you would be unlikely to guess that the person on the other end of the phone was a headhunter. Non-threatening, casual conversations mean that people are happy to talk about their job, their role and the organization they work for, and they will often pass on valuable information to the headhunter, who may very well be considering the speaker as a possible candidate.

Headhunters will usually contact a company three or four times before they actually talk openly to the highlighted individuals within it. The reason for this is the headhunter wants to gain as much insight into the nature and culture of the business as a whole and the possible candidates before making a direct approach. It is also far easier to obtain this information and to make the necessary checks if people aren't fully aware of the situation. In addition, time is of the essence to the headhunter, who needs to do all the necessary research and cannot afford to be put off the scent or go off on a wild goose chase.

SEEKING HONEST RESPONSES

When carrying out their initial research, headhunters telephone people within the targeted company and refer to themselves as journalists, academics or market researchers needing some vital information. With an approach of this kind people tend to give the caller the true facts and figures, rather than saying what they think they should say or fabricating the truth in order to make themselves appear in a better light. This approach helps the headhunter to build up a complete and honest picture of certain organizations and people, which is vital if the headhunter is to pick out the key candidates.

If you are contacted in this way for information, always be helpful and informative but not suspicious. Present your best side – you never know you may hear from this caller again.

Receiving the call

When the headhunter has carried out all the necessary research, the next stage is to approach the potential candidates direct. The candidates receiving the call may be:

- Flattered to be considered, but not interested in the available position.

- Interested in the position, but lacking the necessary qualifications.

- Interested in the position and have all the qualifications, but unhappy with some element of the package.

- Quite interested in the position, but unsure about the implications of a job move.

Any of these can affect the way in which the person responds to the call itself. For example, some candidates are taken aback or indifferent when they receive a call from a headhunter because they aren't expecting it, while others receive so many calls from headhunters that they can be arrogant and therefore extremely difficult for headhunters to deal with.

If you receive a call from a headhunter, the key is to remain calm, take your time and listen to what is being said rather than reacting to what you hear. Listed below are a few tips to help you overcome the emotions of surprise, flattery or excitement, and to help you to focus on the conversation and promoting yourself.

- **Talk in private.** Always make sure you can talk in private. Close your door, direct the call to another extension or take the headhunter's number and call back later. Headhunters understand that it is difficult for people to talk to them when they are at work, especially in an open-plan office, and they will often ring you back on your home telephone number.

- **State your position.** Normally a headhunter will start the conversation by giving you their company and personal name. Next, he/she will brief you on the position itself and then give an outline of the company, indicating whether it is international or national, plc, limited or partnership. However, the headhunter will not disclose the name of the client until he/she meets you in order to ensure confidentiality. Once the headhunter has given you a brief resumé, he/she will turn the conversation around to find out about you.

It is always worth doing a good sales job on yourself. If you are interested in the job, say so. Then go on to sell yourself so that you will get the opportunity of an interview with the headhunter in order to learn more about the job and its responsibilities, profile and prospects. On the other hand, if the job doesn't interest you or is totally unsuitable for whatever reason, don't fall into the trap of switching off or being rude. It is not a good idea to close a door on a potential job source, as you never know when the headhunter *will* have a suitable job for you. Instead, be polite but direct. Tell the headhunter what you currently do, what you are good at and what you have achieved within your current role. Then state what you are looking for from your next career move.

Finally, if you are interested in the position but concerned about one or two issues, either bring these up now if they are fairly major points, or try to negotiate more favourable terms at the initial interview if they are relatively minor. In short, be up front with the headhunter about your exact position in order to avoid wasting everybody's time.

- **Take the lead.** To avoid letting this job opportunity slip away, take charge by asking the headhunter to explain something in more detail or to go over something again if you misheard or misunderstood it. If you are unsure as to whether you have answered the question adequately or given enough information, then ask whether you need to expand on any aspect. Be informative and businesslike; avoid being chatty, pushy or blasé.

- **Engage the prospect.** Every headhunter will be different, but as you have been given an opportunity to talk you don't want to be passed over. In order to arouse the headhunter's interest in you and maintain that level of interest, try to talk the same language. For example, when the headhunter tells you about the job or the company, jot down a few notes or store them in your memory; then, when it is your turn to talk refer to these by saying something like: 'You mentioned earlier that your client is looking for a self-motivated, ambitious leader. I have demonstrated this throughout my career by ......' In this way, as well as keeping the headhunter interested, you are demonstrating your ability to listen and to assimilate information.

- **Stick to the truth.** Most people tell white lies, stretching the truth a bit by adding a bit of additional information, exaggerating the facts or changing the emphasis slightly. This is easy to do, but it is not worth it – it will be only a matter of time before you slip up. Always tell the truth, because not only is it far easier for you to remember what you have said, but you will also build trustworthy relationships.

- **Sell yourself.** Now is your chance to sell yourself. The headhunter wants to hear how good you are at your job and how well regarded you are, so do not be shy, embarrassed or reticent. Tell the headhunter about all your capabilities, skills and achievements. However, being a successful, confident and promotable person doesn't mean just saying that you are: it means talking in terms of your track record and successes to date, referring to things that you have done in your job which distinguish you from your colleagues and predecessors, and backing up your statements with facts and figures to give a clear indication of your level of expertise. For example, the following statement demonstrates the range of someone's marketing skills: 'I have increased sales by 30 per cent in one year by organizing and controlling a £2 million advertising programme'.
  Headhunters will talk to a great many people when they are looking to fill a job, so the key to success is to make yourself stand out from the rest of the candidates by being different or memorable in some way. Some people achieve this by comparing themselves to a well-known or famous

person; for example, instead of referring to yourself simply as an accountant, you might prefer to say, 'In many ways I am the Scrooge of the accounting profession!' Choose a quality you want to portray and find someone to compare yourself to.

Bear in mind that the headhunter will also want to sell the job to all possible candidates, so you need to know what you want from your next career move in order to establish whether this job fits into your career plan. If you don't focus on this you can end up doing more of the same in your new job whether you like doing it or not! Stick to your career plan and you won't be lead astray.

- **Be enthusiastic, helpful and interesting.** Enthusiasm generates energy and positive feelings, so talk enthusiastically about your current role and job. Remember that the tone of your voice is a real indication of what you are really saying. Lowering your voice at the end of a sentence conveys strength and conviction whereas raising your voice reveals an element of uncertainty and converts a statement into a question.

  Try also to be helpful and interesting, but avoid giving long-winded replies. If the job doesn't suit you, suggest the names of people you know who might be interested – someone may do the same for you one day.

Apply the above principles and you will promote yourself as a charismatic, skilled individual who is worthy of a place on the shortlist of suitable candidates.

SEVEN

Getting on to the Shortlist

The headhunter's job is to create a shortlist of potential candidates for the client. This is achieved by researching the market, identifying key people and then determining their suitability by carrying out a telephone interview, assessing their CVs and finally by interviewing them. In order to be awarded a place on the headhunter's shortlist you therefore need to compile a dynamic CV and be prepared to answer some detailed questions. A headhunter's own reputation depends upon the quality of the candidates put forward, so expect every aspect of your job and personality to be probed and assessed. Very often, the true test of knowledge of an interviewer is to ask him/herself whether he/she knows everything about the candidate in the same way as he/she knows everything about a good friend. The key is therefore to prepare in advance but, more importantly, be yourself.

Preparing a dynamic CV

Headhunters and potential employers will need to see your CV. This document should really promote and sell you, at the same time providing detailed information about your current and past experience. Take your time over producing a quality CV. If the headhunter wants to see it urgently, then negotiate an extra few days in order to revamp your current one – there is absolutely no point in throwing away a job opportunity on account of a poor CV.

A dynamic CV is one which arouses the employer's interest in you and convinces him/her to invite you to attend an interview. However, most CVs are of a poor standard, being full of errors, poorly presented and produced in a rush. If you can market yourself professionally and effectively, you will distinguish yourself from the competition and therefore make your CV work for you.

A CV is dynamic if it makes the employer's job easy. It should include everything the employer wants to see, be written in the employer's language and be professionally presented. Most CVs, however, make very dull reading, so apply the following principles in order to make your CV stand out from the crowd.

1 **Target your CV towards the job on offer.** To do this, put yourself in the employer's shoes and think about what he/she is looking for. For example, what experience, technical knowledge or type of person is the employer searching for? Once you have decided these basic facts write your CV, focusing and expanding upon the key issues to demonstrate your suitability for the job.

2 **Include a capabilities section.** This should appear on the first page and is the crux of a dynamic CV, because it gives candidates the opportunity to sell themselves, their capabilities and their life experiences to the employer. Most CVs don't include a capabilities section and therefore sell only the candidates' previous experience rather than their whole potential. Some of the details in this section may be repeated again in the employment history section. However, there is no harm in this as long as it is phrased in a different way, and it will make the CV more memorable.

Choose about four capability headings. One will be a technical and the others perhaps managerial, leadership, communication, training, systems or anything which is applicable to the job. Under each heading include four or five sentences, each explaining a different one of your skills, in order to give the employer an idea of your potential. Remember that a capability doesn't have to be something you have enormous experience of but something you know you can do. Try also to demonstrate a range of competence, so include both basic and difficult skills.

3 **Highlight your qualifications.** Qualifications are important because they provide the employer with concrete assurances that the person is qualified to do the job on offer. However, the problem with most qualification sections is that they are difficult to understand and follow. The simple rules are:

- Indicate your most recent qualifications first.

- Highlight the level of the qualification in bold, then in ordinary type show the subject, grade, establishment and date achieved.

- Put internal or external job training courses in a separate section. It is best to highlight these in the employment history section under the relevant job.

4 **Give an indication of your personality.** Most CVs are faceless and it is not until the employer actually meets the candidate that he/she gains an insight into their personality. Avoid this trap at all costs. The headhunter may already have given you an indication of what type of person the employer is seeking, but if you don't know then ask. Include your personality details under a personal heading in the capabilities section. Choose anything which is applicable to you, but try to make it relevant to the work situation. For example, instead of saying simply that you work hard, write instead: 'Hardworking and task-orientated. Leave when the job is done rather than when it is time to go home'. In this way you can emphasize and highlight what is important to you.

5 **Emphasize your achievements.** Achievements count, so list them all under the employment section – they can turn an ordinary candidate into an outstanding one. An achievement is anything which you have done as part of or over and above the job specification. It doesn't have to be earth shattering, just something which shows that you have succeeded in the job and can contribute to the organizations you work for.

Spend time on producing a really good CV. Never lie, fabricate or include something simply for the sake of it. And remember that if an employer is prepared to invest in you, it is worth you investing in a dynamic CV. (For further details on writing a CV, refer to *How to Write a Perfect CV in a Weekend*, also in this series.)

Preparing for interview

The next step is to prepare some topics for the interview. The key here is to research the subject in advance so that you are confident in answering questions, but to avoid preparing answers to specific questions. The danger with this is that the particular questions may not crop up, in which case you could become flustered, lose confidence or, worse still, give your prepared answer anyway. Alternatively, if the questions are asked you could just sound unreal – employers want candidates to be themselves, so you should prepare but not rehearse answers.

Listed below are some topics which could crop up in your interview. Read through the possible questions and think about your own particular qualities. Gain some insight into yourself and think about how you would respond if someone asked you some of these questions.

1 Staying Power. This is important, because the employer wants to establish whether or not the appointed person will stay in the job long enough for the money invested in him/her to show a return. It is also vital for an employer to know how much supervision a person requires: can you be relied upon to start and finish a task with minimal supervision, or do you require a lot of direction and nurturing?

If staying power has been a problem for you, then be prepared to explain this and give positive reasons why it is the case, rather than glossing over it or putting it down to a change of mind or plan. The aim is to reassure the interviewer that staying power is not a problem for you *now*. The headhunter can establish how much staying power you have by asking:

- How long do you intend to stay in the job on offer?

- How long have you remained in previous jobs, and what caused you to make a move?

- What made you stop your education/training or fail to complete a course?

- How stable are your personal relationships?

- What is your attitude towards disappointment: try again to ensure success, put it behind you, or to take it to heart?

2 Working hard. Employers want to hire committed, hard-working people who can apply themselves to give their best. In short, they are after doers not talkers. The headhunter will probe to discover how much energy you have for hard work by asking:

- What have you changed, improved or done in addition to your job specification?

- How often do you find yourself with nothing to do?

- How have you displayed initiative in your current role?

- How would you describe your job's objectives: as a challenge, achievable with hard work, or easily achievable?

3 Degree of selfishness. Employers expect the company's interests to be put before those of their employees. An employer wants to hire someone who is willing to work as part of the overall team in order to achieve the company's objectives. The headhunter can gauge your degree of selfishness by asking:

- What do yo think of such and such person? The head-hunter will be interested to see whether you can give praise where praise is due or whether you criticize or cut other people down at the first opprtunity. The way you respond will give an indication of your perception of others in relation to yourself.

- How would you respond if you were asked to perform something outside your job specification? Here the headhunter is looking to see whether there is an element of give and take and a willingness to muck in and help others, or whether you think purely about yourself.

4 Sociability. Employers want to hire people who accept others and build relationships with everyone. The headhunter can establish whether you like people and are liked by others by asking:

- What kinds of relationships do you have with people in your current job?

- Is there anyone you can't get along with?

- What are your family relationships like?

- Do you prefer to work on your own or with others?

5 Independence. Employees need to be able to do things for themselves rather than relying too heavily on others for help or guidance. The headhunter can guage the level of your independence by asking:

- How comfortable are you with making your own decisions?

- How do you discover new things; for yourself, or do you wait to be told?

- How would you describe your financial position: independent, or dependent upon your partner or family?

6 Leadership. Organizations rely upon leaders to inspire others. A good leader earns the trust and respect of those around him/her and can offer advice and help to others. The headhunter can determine your leadership qualities by asking:

- How do you persuade others to your way of thinking?

- How is your leadership interpreted by others?

- Who is the leader at home?

- What are your key leadership qualities?

- Would you describe others as trusting or fearing you?

7 Motivation. This is vital in the business environment. Motivation is the force within each person which drives them to work better, harder or faster than others. Employers want to have motivated individuals who are hungry for success. The headhunter can determine how motivated you are by asking:

- How important is money to you?

- Are you reliant upon this job in order to survive, or do you have another private income?

- Is this an ideal job for you or the means to another, more suitable job?

- How committed are you to achieving your goals?

8 Maturity. An employer needs to establish whether or not a candidate has the degree of maturity required for the job on offer. Maturity is difficult to determine, because it is often only when an individual is put in a particular situation that the level of their maturity is displayed. It has more to do with how a person perceives things than with how the person appears to others. Maturity includes:

- Being independent.

- Accepting responsibilities.

- Stating the truth, even if it is unpleasant for the recipient.

- The ability to share.

- Understanding the consequences of your actions.

- Being in control and disciplined.

- Being able to explain things to others without showing off, winding them up or putting them down.

The headhunter may ask questions which force you to think on your feet in order to try to determine your degree of maturity.

9 Technical capabilities. Having employees with the right level of experience and expertise is vital for an employer, so expect the headhunter to ask detailed questions about your duties, responsibilities and technical experience. Try to give informative yet succinct answers, and where possible give examples. Include information which enhances your case and can be passed on to the employer.

10 Achievements. Employers want to employ achievers rather than just doers, so, the headhunter will ask you what you have achieved within your jobs to date.

Think about all your achievements in advance and make a mental note of them. Practise talking aloud about your achievements in order to get used to hearing yourself communicate your value. Make yourself look a winner and focus on things you have improved, implemented, saved, changed, instructed, managed, designed and so on. In fact, mention anything which demonstates the value of your contribution to an organization.

Practice makes perfect, and it will then be easier for you to recall and talk about your achievements to the headhunter or employer with confidence and conviction.

The headhunter may also question you on any failures. The key is to try to turn a negative situation into a positive one by talking in terms of what the experiences taught you or how it made you grow as a person. Avoid dwelling on negative issues or blaming others, but be big enough to admit responsibility where necessary.

The headhunter will thus question every aspect of your personal and professional life in order to find the candidate most suited to the job on offer. To do this, the headhunter may ask you to solve problems to see how well you can think on your feet, or challenge your answers to see whether you can justify your opinions. Enter into the spirit of the situation and avoid taking offence or becoming hostile or aggressive. If you can be yourself and maintain your sense of humour, you will win through and be put on the headhunter's shortlist of candidates.

EIGHT

If the Headhunter doesn't Call

Headhunters search out the best and make it their business to know what people are doing. However, despite your expertise and brilliance you may not yet have received that call from a headhunter. The truth is that it is still rare for people to be headhunted and even the most eligible candidates may receive only one call from a headhunter within their entire career – and this may not even be for the right kind of job. The key to success is therefore not to wait for the headhunter to call you but to start promoting yourself. Refer to Chapters 3 and 4 to help you build both an internal and an external reputation in order to increase your career options.

'You are being watched!' This chapter deals with the issue of internal self-promotion, for it is more likely that your current employer will headhunt you than that an agency will. People often disregard the importance of their existing employer and underestimate their power to select and poach people for promotion. You can therefore improve your business opportunities by performing your current role better than you do it now, and listed below are a few tips to help you.

- **Focus on the important issues.** Spend some time thinking about the fundamental requirements of your job. Most people don't do this, but spend most of their time on the unimportant things by making them appear important and urgent. To find out how important something is, ask yourself what its purpose is – then judge the importance of the task by your answer.

  Important work is high-priority work, so increase your performance by spending 80 per cent of your time on the priorities and leave or delegate the low-priority work. Sometimes by putting low-priority work to one side, the need for it to be done at all disappears. Concentrate on the essentials and your job satisfaction will increase, because there is now a definite purpose to your work. Adopting this approach also means that you will be valued more highly.

- **Make an impact.** Focus on making an impact in your job. Establish what you can do in your work that would create the greatest impact in the least amount of time. Maybe there is a particular task that you have avoided, not completed or put on hold – now is the time to do it. Spend your time wisely to make your own individual mark.

- **Do a bit extra.** People notice others who perform only the duties in their job specification. Take on more work or tasks in order to gain experience, support others and to demonstrate your potential.

- **Let things go.** Learn to let certain things go or not make an issue out of something that is not worth it. Avoid playing politics or games, or taking sides. Instead of fighting against the system, understand how it works and use it to your advantage. Fighting is time consuming and energy sapping, so focus your energy on what is important and avoid getting worked up over insignificant issues (once the fighting stops, it is easier for those people who are left to recognize how unimportant an issue really is). Try to gain attention for yourself from focusing on the right sorts of issues.

- **Be prepared to go it alone.** You may not always receive the support you require for one of your ideas. Recognize that sometimes people refuse to support others for the wrong kinds of reasons such as jealousy, pride and self-esteem. However, you are your own person, so trust your ideas, beliefs and convictions. Realize that there is no harm in going out on a limb or doing something which has never been attempted before. Trust your own instincts, but put in adequate preparation. Remember that some of the greatest achievements ever have been solo ones.

- **Attend essential meetings.** Your time is precious, so attend only essential meetings. Reducing your appearances also means that others start to value your time and input far more. Focus on the purpose of the meeting: if you can't contribute much, then don't attend. A meeting should also be effective, so consider how many people will be attending – if there will be more than five or six, productivity will decrease. Under these circumstances it is often a good idea to show up for part of the time, to present your issue but avoid the chit-chat at the beginning and end of the meeting.

- **Prepare for meetings.** Command attention and respect by being prepared. Attending a meeting unprepared is a grave mistake, and this means *every* meeting, even the departmental ones. Here, many people turn up unprepared because they are in the presence of friends or colleagues, but this is the very time to make your capabilities known. Avoid sitting back or letting others do all the talking; instead, prepare things in advance – perhaps a few slides or hand-outs – take control of the situation, and show your superiors and colleagues that you are someone who has great potential.

- **Assess yourself regularly.** Assess your performance regularly with a view to improving it. A contact of mine told me how he sat down each week to assess his previous week's performance. He noted what had gone well and what needed to be improved. The purpose of this exercise was to strive continuously for a better performance rather than simply criticizing himself for the lack of one.

- **Give yourself time off.** Ensure that you have enough 'self' time to enjoy yourself. Take time out in order to recharge your batteries and give yourself the time to think. Accept that there *is* time to do what you want to do!

- **Promote your best image.** You want to be the best, so give your best. Watch, notice and try to be different to those around you. Don't follow – lead.

Follow these principles in order to make your employer interested in you. Develop, shape and promote your own reputation, so that in future your employer chooses *you*.

NINE

Conclusion

Do everything you can to enjoy your job and be good at it, and you will then stand every chance of being headhunted. Make quality your passion, manage your time, and enlist enough love and support from those around you to help you cope with all your pressures, demands and responsibilities. Try to create a purpose to your life and career, rather than making everything a chore. Finally, take time out for fun and physical activity in order to stay in shape and remain alert. You owe it to yourself to have the best possible choices in the demanding and relentless business world, where only the best people survive long term. Remember, this life is the real thing – not a rehearsal.

Be the best at what you do and be open to change and new career initiatives. Try consciously to build up your reputation in your field of work and continuously promote yourself, for then your reputation will lead the way. A contact recently told me how a director of a well-known company flew abroad to attend a job interview. However, the director's interview with a competitor organization was discovered by a co-director, who was flying to the same destination on holiday when he noticed the collection board in the arrival hall bearing the name of his colleague. When the director subsequently handed in his notice to the managing director, he was surprised to find that the managing director already knew what organization he was joining. Well-known, key people command a lot of interest and attention, and their reputation follows them wherever they go!

Listed opposite are a few key reminders to help you to build your reputation and increase your potential to be headhunted. Refer back to this list regularly as a reminder of the ways to enhance your career.

1 Have a vision. A vision of your career and its path helps to focus the mind and create positive feelings. It ensures that your career is driven by the vision itself and not by emotion; it helps you to weather the plateau periods, take jobs that enhance your career not your pocket, and avoid any irrational job moves. Recognize the value of a vision.

2 Perform a quality job. Focus on achieving within your current role and being recognized for your achievements. People are judged on what they do, not on what they meant to do, so care about your work – because if you don't, others will.

3 Become visible. Headhunters look for candidates in the press and professional and academic institutes, and they also talk to their contacts within commerce, industry and social establishments. You need to be visible and talk about yourself and your job.

    ● **Talk about yourself.** This carries a risk, but if you don't talk about yourself, who will? When you talk to people, demonstrate your value and, when necessary, give yourself the credit. Balance revealing too much about yourself against being too protective. Assess every situation as it arises and use your discretion.

    ● **Talk about your job.** Are you proud of what you do? If not, why not? Make a conscious effort to pass on your name, profession and company when you are introduced to someone. Tell people what you do and how well you do it. It is the easiest way to become known within your profession.

4 Create your own trademark. Decide what you want to be recognized for and then talk about yourself in this way. Control and manage your own publicity.

5 Know yourself. Headhunters and employers will want to know all about you in detail, so get to know yourself. Understand what motivates you and drives you forward. Get a feel for what you want to do more of or less of.

⑥ Develop a positive attitude. A positive person who is open and friendly and says and does what he/she wants to do. Be aware of what you are communicating to others about yourself, both verbally and through your body language. Refresh your attitude and decouple yourself from work demands by:

> ● **Taking time out for yourself.** Everyone needs time to reflect, and to refresh and enjoy themselves. You can take this time first thing in the morning, last thing at night, or between meetings. Protect yourself from anxiety and stress.

> ● **Valuing yourself.** Others will only value you if you value yourself. Recognize and appreciate your qualities and strengths.

> ● **Paying attention to your thoughts.** What do you think about? Are your thoughts positive and pleasant, or negative and destructive? When you start thinking negatively, stop yourself and turn the thought into a positive one.

Changing the habits of a lifetime is hard, but it may be necessary in order to build a reputation which is highly sought after. You need to recognize that you hold the key to your future success.

Knowing how to be headhunted doesn't automatically ensure success. It is up to you to create your own business initiatives and to promote yourself continuously in every way possible. Then you will encourage people to start knocking on *your* door in the future.

Index